My Wild Life

With best wishes

[signature]

My Wild Life

Simon Cowell

with

Nick Harding

Michael O'Mara Books Limited

First published in Great Britain in 2016 by
Michael O'Mara Books Limited
9 Lion Yard
Tremadoc Road
London SW4 7NQ

A CIP catalogue record for this book is available from the
British Library.

Papers used by Michael O'Mara Books Limited are natural, recyclable
products made from wood grown in sustainable forests. The
manufacturing processes conform to the environmental regulations of
the country of origin.

ISBN: 978-1-78243-520-4 in hardback print format
ISBN: 978-1-78243-522-8 in ebook format

1 2 3 4 5 6 7 8 9 10

www.mombooks.com

Cover design by Richard Green
Designed and typeset by K DESIGN, Winscombe, Somerset

Printed and bound by CPI Group (UK) Ltd, Croydon, CR0 4YY

Contents

Oh, Deer

SOMETIMES YOU GET lucky and the caller gives you accurate information so you can make an educated assessment of the situation and give the poor creature caught at the sharp end of the emergency a fighting chance. In any rescue there are always variables so instinct and experience play a big part. I'm certainly no Dr Dolittle but I do get a sense of what most of the animals I rescue are feeling by their body language and the way they behave. This empathy is the difference between a successful outcome or blundering into a situation, spooking an animal into a panic and creating even more danger for it.

When the caller is an animal expert it makes the job easier because usually they know what they are talking about, as was the case one sunny day in 2013 when the phone in the office rang and the RSPCA was on the other end of the line.

'It's a roe deer and it's trapped in a car park . . . in a school . . . in the middle of south London,' the guy explained. 'It's got some kind of facial injury. There is a lot of blood. The police are here too and the deer is really panicked. The school is near a main road and the kids have been kept inside but I don't know how long it will stay here. If it gets out it could cause a major accident.'

I shuddered to think of the carnage that an adult deer would cause on a busy London road.

'I'm on my way. Let me know if the situation changes,' I told the caller.

Then, with the familiar adrenaline buzz firing my synapses, I jumped out my chair and ran over to the store room to grab the equipment we'd need for the rescue. Top of the list was the huge net we kept for large, fast animals. If the deer was going to bolt from wherever it was, we would need something to stop it getting onto the road.

'Lucy,' I yelled. 'Emergency!'

By the time I got to the car Wildlife Aid's trusty vet nurse was waiting along with one of our volunteers who was also acting as cameraman. I knew I would need an experienced team and I called my number-two rescuer, Sean, who lived nearby and was every bit as good as I was. We loaded up the Volvo and sped out of the gates. Less than four minutes had elapsed since I'd hung up. I started to work things out in my head. Deer rescues were tricky: the animals are big, fast and unpredictable. To successfully corner and catch a deer you need enough people to close off all the exits. There were three of us in the car, at least one RSPCA officer and some police officers. Hopefully that would be enough.

No two rescues are the same and every rescue presents its own special set of circumstances. Each species has its own behavioural traits and quirks and each individual animal has its own personality. Some are bold and aggressive, some are frightened and shy. Very rarely, some seem to know that you are there to help and passively allow you to do what you need to do in order to save them.

Deer are tricky customers, which is why the RSPCA called us. They are terrified of man and want to get away from you. You need to be extremely careful and extremely quick when the capture moment presents itself. You can't afford mistakes, both for the sake of the deer and for the sake of the rescuer. Antlers hurt, believe me. I've been caught twice by them, once in the forehead and once in the neck. You also have to watch their hooves because a deer can jump several feet from standing and has a hell of a lot of latent energy stored in its legs. One kick can easily rupture an organ.

Deer can also cause all kinds of harm to themselves when they are in flight mode. They are prone to stress and shock and roe deer are the only deer that can develop a condition called capture myopathy, which is an acute condition with symptoms varying from muscle stiffness to paralysis, respiratory problems and cardiac arrest. They can literally get scared to death.

I arrived at the school and was met by two RSPCA officers in uniform: a man and a woman. The school was on lock-down and excited faces stared out of each window. I scanned the L-shaped car park and spied the deer – a roe buck with large antlers – cowering behind a car at one end of it. It was panting, its flanks were streaked with sweat and speckled with blood from a deep wound in its mouth. I couldn't see the extent of the injury but even from a distance the amount of blood suggested it was serious.

There were around twenty cars parked in spaces with enough room around them for the deer to dart through, which meant it would be hard to catch. The car park was bordered on several sides by the brick school buildings and also by the playground, which was enclosed by a high chain-link fence, so while there was room for the animal to run around, there was only one exit – the opening to the road. There were borders and some trees on the fringes of the car park too.

The male RSPCA officer introduced himself.

'What's the situation and why haven't you gone for it?' I asked. 'You are worrying me now.' He explained that he had sought advice from the agency Natural England who had told him simply to catch and release the deer but that the police had wisely vetoed the plan in case the release caused a traffic accident. Bemused, I asked whether English Nature had given any tips on how they assumed the deer would be caught in the first place.

'Do you just say "come here, deer", put it in the car and drive off?' I joked.

I knew we needed to get the deer in a position where it would have no option but to run through the net. Once caught I could grab it, sedate it and then gauge what medical attention was needed. Before any of that happened, however, I needed to work out where to release it. Once we had it under sedation we would need to treat it and release it quickly, preferably back to where it had come from. I looked at a map of the local area. The only likely open space was a small area of woodland around half a mile away. If all went well that would be our final destination.

I began to work out the logistics of the rescue. We needed two net holders and several herders to gently corral the animal into a corner. The net was around 6 metres wide and could be extended to around 2.5 metres high if you held it above your head. We could form a barrier with it between two cars parked opposite each other.

The sun was beating down as I started to place each person at strategic points and direct them backwards and forwards towards the deer, then away when it got spooked. I spoke quietly and used hand signals to issue commands. On several occasions the deer broke cover from where it was cowering and darted behind cars and past rescuers. I was careful not to encourage anyone to make a lunge and try to grab it. It may have been scared and exhausted but it still had plenty of energy and the more it felt threatened, the more agitated it would become. We made several slow passes up and down the car park in a game of cat and mouse where the mouse was a terrified 20 kg deer. At one tantalizing pass the deer sped past Lucy, close enough for her to touch it.

'Don't try,' I said as it streaked past her. It would have been foolhardy and dangerous to attempt to grab the antlers when the animal was going at full pelt.

Eventually, after over an hour of gentle manoeuvring, we

got the animal in a position where I felt capture was possible. It was cornered in the far end of the car park with a wall behind it and two cars parked opposite each other creating a bottleneck through which it had to run. The net holders positioned themselves at either side of the gap, holding the net up at maximum height. Lucy stood back ready to tranquillize the animal when it became entangled. I walked slowly in front of the net. The deer knew it couldn't go any further back and made a bolt to try and get past me. It saw the net at the last second and tried to leap over it. Its antlers got caught and in that split second I pounced and grabbed the horns in my gloved hands, taking care to keep them away from anywhere they could do damage. I wrestled it to the ground and the RSPCA officers jumped in to help. A terrified, guttural grunt rang out across the car park as the poor thing was pinned to the tarmac. We needed to restrain it for its own safety but it didn't understand. It just wanted to escape.

Lucy ran into the melee and administered the sedative. A vet had arrived and oversaw the injection. Slowly the deer's terrified pants became more laboured and it slumped as the fight drained from its exhausted body. The relief at getting to that stage was huge. I looked down at the creature in my hands and felt a wave of sadness. The poor thing must have been terrified. I made a promise that I would do all I could to get it back to safety. Then I saw the wound in its mouth. Its lower lip was split completely in a deep V-shape which sliced down its chin to its jawline. Blood was seeping from the wound onto the ground.

'This is going to need several stitches and antibiotics,' I said.

We travel with sedatives and other supplies but we did not have a suture kit that day.

'Lucy, you'll need to find a local vet and get what you need to deal with the wound,' I said and looked at my watch. 'It's ten to three now, we've got an hour.'

Once you sedate an animal, you have a time window because you can't keep it sedated forever. The deer was in a state of shock and even under sedation I could feel its heart pumping quickly. I didn't want to keep it under for any longer than an hour. Lucy ran off with one of the RSPCA officers to find a local vet while the other officer and I gently lifted the deer off the tarmac and to a shaded, grassy area where I covered its eyes with some gauze and lay quietly with it, waiting anxiously. Every few minutes I checked its heart rate. To begin with it was strong but as fifteen minutes passed, and then thirty, the rhythm began to get less regular and the animal's breathing slowed.

By fifty minutes the heart beat had become very erratic, speeding up then stopping for a couple of beats. The deer was dying. I stroked its face gently and it began to convulse. I thought that was it. I thought it was going into death throes. I could feel the life slowly drain from it.

I looked up across the car park and saw a white car pull in. The door opened and Lucy got out with a local vet who needed to oversee the medical side of the operation; a vision in green scrubs. She sprinted over and quickly stitched the wound and administered a long-lasting antibiotic. We lifted the animal into the back of the Volvo. Time was critical. I sat in the car with our patient and we sped off into the

London traffic to the release site, which was less than a kilometre away.

We were at the site within five minutes and two of us lifted the deer and half walked, half ran with it to get it as far from the road as possible. The site was a large park with playing fields and woodland beyond. We got the deer to the edge of the woods and laid it on the grass.

Lucy knelt down with a syringe of antidote at the ready. She plunged the needle into the animal's haunch, reversed the sedation and after about thirty seconds the deer came back to life, full of strength and the natural urge to get as far away from me and the other humans as possible. It stood and I pointed it in the right direction. Once it was facing forward I let go.

It was unsure at first but became fully alert and leapt over the escarpment that formed a natural border between the fields and the woodland. It was one of the most glorious sights I have ever seen. I watched as it bounded to freedom while the lady from the RSPCA pumped her fists in jubilation next to me. Then the tears came. I always shed them when I see an animal go back to the wild.

'It deserves a second chance,' I sobbed. All the adrenaline and the fears that had kept me going that day dissipated and I slumped into the grass and cried like a baby as another satisfied customer disappeared into the urban jungle.

Beyond the trees, in the distance, the London skyline spread across the horizon like a mirage. Once, in another life symbolized by fast cars, casinos, bad behaviour, money and excess, that landscape had been my stalking ground.

How the hell did I get here? I thought to myself.

CHAPTER ONE

In the Beginning There Was Simon

MY STORY STARTS like all good wildlife stories with a baby creature covered in hair, mewling and whining in its mother's protective embrace. It is a mancub and it is me, Simon Cowell (no not that one, although I'm pretty sure he would have been an equally hirsute newborn). I was a tiny infant and entered the world prematurely weighing just two pounds after my mother suffered a pre-pregnancy bout of tuberculosis. Despite the freakish dark pelt that covered me at birth but cruelly deserted me prematurely in later life, I was a handsome devil and a plucky little fighter loved by the nurses. They crowned me King Simon and fussed over me in the drab post-war maternity unit of Epsom General Hospital. The magnetic chemistry I shared with the opposite sex as a baby was something I tried to maintain in my formative years, often at personal cost.

Before I came along my mum, Jeanne, had lost a child: another boy. I suspect that after I arrived in such dramatic fashion and gave her and my dad, Michael, a fright, they decided to cut their reproductive losses and quit while they were ahead. Consequently, I remained an only child (I like to think I was a blessing), and that suited me fine.

I was born in April 1952 and my habitat was the idyllic surroundings of Surrey and, in particular, Epsom, a market town made famous by the racecourse and the world's largest cluster of psychiatric hospitals. They had been built at the turn of the twentieth century to provide a centralized hub in which to house and treat the nation's growing community of mentally ill and insane people. Some were let out at the weekends, which made the Saturday shop interesting. Often in later life I felt like joining them and on a couple of occasions I nearly did, but more of that later.

Dad came from an agricultural family and grew up in a village called Radwinter in Essex, which was a rural backwater. During the Second World War he left the farm and joined the RAF where he served as an engineer and was posted to Singapore and Burma. He fixed aircraft and was bloody good at it thanks to years spent tinkering with tractors and other heavy machinery in the farm workshop. He was an extraordinary handyman with a sixth sense that allowed him to understand how machines worked. He was still in the Far East when the Japanese surrendered in 1945 and was part of the liberation effort that went into the prisoner-of-war camps and helped repatriate the wretched souls who survived. I can only imagine the sights he witnessed in those chaotic weeks. He never talked about it to me or anyone else and put his dark memories in a box somewhere in his head and locked them away. He was a great bloke and the backbone of the family.

After the war he worked for a farm supply wholesaler in Dorking as an engineer and also sold big plant such as tractors and combine harvesters. His clients were farmers and farm managers and he'd broker deals worth several thousand pounds. If I was off school or on holiday he sometimes took me with him on business. There was a workshop at his business premises where I was allowed to mess around with the tools and the machinery. There were none of the silly health and safety regulations that strangle the fun out of life nowadays. It was a time of innocence and the occasional industrial accident!

When I was a few years old we moved further out into the countryside to a village called Brockham which was a pretty place with a village green and a church that sat in the shadow of Box Hill. Dad went to work; Mum stayed at home and looked after me and the house. All told we were an unremarkable post-war family.

I went to Leigh County Primary School, which my parents chose over the nearest school to our home. My mother had aspirations to be a social climber and didn't feel that the local school was good enough for me, so I suffered the longer walk to further my academic potential (which never really materialized). By chance several of my teachers lived on my road so I always had to be on my best behaviour. There was Miss Keen, the headmistress who terrified the life out of me, and Miss Collinson who had a tin leg. She lived with a lady friend, Miss Smith. Both were sweet, middle-aged ladies (although Miss Collinson was a little bit scary because of the leg) and I was blissfully ignorant about their living arrangements. To this day, I have no idea whether they were just friends or friends with benefits. They were always lovely to me and, perhaps because I was a neighbour, Miss Collinson always looked out for me in school. One day I remember getting a really bad earache and snivelling in pain during class. Miss Collinson came and got me from my desk and gently led me to the front of the room where she placed a little chair next to her for me to sit on. As she taught the rest of the class she encouraged me to rest my head in her ample lap where the cold tin of her prosthetic limb soothed away my pain through the linen of her dress.

Finally, there was Mr Booth who lived next door with his wife. He was a keen amateur photographer and gave me my first camera. Later I developed an interest in photographing birds (of the feathered kind) and Mr Booth became my mentor.

There weren't a lot of people my age in my life. I suspect Mum kept me away from other children to stop me from getting distracted from my school work. Being an only child and a solitary one at that, I didn't have friends round to play and, like my parents, I wasn't social.

Mum and Dad were both protective of me; they doted on me and probably cosseted me too much, turning me into a close approximation of the classic only child. We never really talked about our feelings as a family. If there was a problem, it got dealt with and we moved on without the need for analysis or reflection. We certainly didn't get into the murky business of emotions, which were a Rubicon that was never crossed. You dealt with them on your own. Even now I tend not to show my emotions to people. It is only when I am with animals that I allow myself the luxury of emotional expression.

Family life was routine and never dramatic. We went on holiday every year to Fairlight near Hastings where we rented a caravan and would go shrimping, which was a family tradition; the three us wading through the rock pools with nets, silhouetted against the drab English Channel. It was in Fairlight that I learned my first lesson about respect for the animal kingdom courtesy of a flock of geese. I was sent to get some milk from the farm across the way. I was only around five or six at the time and as I plodded down the driveway to the house the animals descended on me in an angry mob. The thing about geese is that although they rear up, flap their wings and make a fuss, if you call their bluff and stand up to them they back down straight away and run off. As a kid I didn't know this and turned around terrified, genuinely fearing for my life. I ran back to our caravan as the flock squawked after me, sensing an easy victory. While Mum soothed me, Dad suppressed a chuckle. He made up for the trauma a few weeks later when he came home with one of the huge wooden crates that a tractor had been delivered in. It was the size of a room and he put it up for me in the garden. It became my shed; I had my own tools on a rack along the wall and I spent hours in there on my own, tinkering away. The crate took on a life of its own in my imagination and became different things; sometimes it was a tank, sometimes a submarine.

As a family we were very much connected to farming. We visited Dad's side of the family fairly regularly, taking the drive to Essex in the family cars we had over the years, which included a Ford Corsair, a Ford Zephyr and a Triumph 2000. I spent most of my summer holidays with my cousin David on my aunt and uncle's farm, where I learned about husbandry and swearing. David and I were close and as a child he was the nearest thing I had to a sibling. I loved farmers and the farm life and later, in my teens, I got work after school and at weekends at local farms near our house.

I've often tried to work out where my empathy and interest in animals came from. Those early experiences of farming had much to do with it, as did family pets we owned over the years. There were also characters in my childhood who shared an interest in wildlife with me. There was Mr Booth and his photography and, in particular, a woman called Anne Cooper who lived up the road. She was as wide as she was tall, had an interesting arrangement of teeth and sported a moustache of which Groucho Marx would have been proud. She was a lovely, eccentric woman who loved wild animals and took them in when they had been injured. We got to know her well and often popped in to have a cup of tea and see what new visitors she had added to the menagerie she called home.

'Come and have a look at this,' she would call as you passed her open front door.

She'd beckon you inside her ramshackle home where the floor was always covered in mud, and in the kitchen she would have foxes or hedgehogs running around or recovering in wire cages. People knew Anne rescued wild animals so they called her if they found a stranded badger or a bird with a broken wing. On the kitchen sideboard she kept a pile of dead rats that she fed to the carnivores and which she'd shove out the way while she prepared her dinner or made tea for visitors. Subliminally, in Anne's kitchen, the seeds of my destiny were undoubtedly sown.

I was a hands-on child, not an academic one, so was amazed, aged eight, when I passed the entrance exam for a private school that my parents were adamant I went to.

On my first day at the City of London Freemen's School, Dad drove and allowed me to sit in the front. My parents were full of pride that morning. Socially, they had arrived! I was the first and to my knowledge the only child in our road to reach such academic heights. I failed to share their enthusiasm, however, and in my blue top and blazer, grey shorts and cap, felt parental expectation weighing down on me. The drive seemed to take an age and when it was time for me to go in and meet my new classmates I locked my fingers around the steering wheel and refused to leave the car. Dad prized me free and gently coaxed me towards what he believed would be a better life.

Freemen's was a good school, the centrepiece of which was an imposing Georgian mansion, and it took in both boarders and day pupils. Luckily I got to return home to the warm bosom of my family each night. I don't know if I would have survived the full-on boarding-school experience.

The student body included the children of wealthy businessmen and public figures. There was plenty of good breeding along with other children who came from normal homes such as mine. It didn't take long for the posh kids to find us out. They just knew when someone wasn't on the same level as them. They could sniff out middle-income spawn and inevitably a hierarchy was established to keep the hoi polloi in its place. At first, the bullying was low level and was directed at plenty of other normal children, too. But in the second or third year something happened that took the attention I got from the bullies to another level. Inexorably and mysteriously I developed a stutter, which set me apart from the other low-ranking children. It shone out like a beacon among the plummy accents. I was S-s-stuttering S-s-Simon, the butt of many j-j-jokes. I struggled and stumbled over words, and then it developed into a physical tic. If I struggled with a word my neck would crick and my head would bend to the side, as with my mouth open and my chin jutting forward I tried to push the troublesome words out. The more aware I became of the impediment, the more it manifested itself.

The stutter stayed with me for many years and defined my identity. In life you get over things and you move on so, looking back now, I can view it with the luxury of cool detachment but at the time it became all-consuming. While I squirmed, did my best not to talk and hated my stutter, the adult world ignored it. My parents never spoke about it, the teachers never spoke about it and I was never sent to a speech therapist (I don't even know if they existed in those days). My stutter became my nemesis and I developed coping mechanisms to conquer it, one of which was to make myself ill.

In class the most terrifying lessons were the ones where pupils were required to read out loud. To me it was pure cruelty. I would listen as the line of pupils sitting in front of me read their pages one by one. As each one finished and the reading got nearer to me, my heart beat faster. I allowed the panic and anxiety to grow inside me and invited the waves of nausea in. I willed myself to pass out. Sweat would pour from me and the fear and terror became intolerable until the teacher noticed and sent me to the sick bay. It happened all the time and the more stressed I got, the more the stutter took hold. If someone said to me all those years ago I would eventually present a TV show I would have laughed.

Maybe it was the stress of those excruciating events that led me towards one of the great love affairs of my life: smoking. Dad smoked like a trooper and although he discouraged me from taking up the habit, which Mum hated, I started when I was about twelve or thirteen. The ciggies lured me in gently at first. I used to cycle from our house to a shop a mile away in a village called Strood Green where I could buy a box of two Olympic cigarettes for sixpence. Purchase complete, I would find a quiet hedge to hide behind and smoke them. It was my little rebellion: those two cigarettes were a two-fingered salute to the rigid rules of my life.

Despite that, I was a healthy child. I was a fit lad and apparently several of the girls at school fancied me. I enjoyed physical pursuits but was not a team player. I would do anything to get out of rugby. As far as I was concerned it was a filthy, dirty game. I liked athletics because that was just me performing on my own. I was more of a short-distance athlete and ran a respectable 100 metres. Any more than that and I tended to need a cigarette. Cricket I quite enjoyed, too, but that was often spoiled by the running gag that I had reached my tic century. Each time I ticked someone would call a six.

I look back on my school days with fondness. I made some good friends, I cracked on and did the stuff I enjoyed. I sang (which wasn't affected by the stutter) and played the trumpet. I took part in school productions and found sanctuary on stage but I couldn't act because I couldn't speak. I was in all the school choirs, performed solo comfortably and took the lead during one of the school music evenings.

I did harbour ambitions to be a vet but it became clear as the years went on that I would never get the required grades. Within reason, if I saw someone do something once I could pretty much do it without help afterwards. I excelled at woodwork and when I was about fifteen Dad handed me my freedom in the form of a scrapped motorcycle. I'd owned a tiny one before, a 30 cc thing with the motor in the back wheel that I screamed around the garden on, but this was a 90 cc James Comet – a proper adult bike.

Mum hated motorbikes so Dad waited until she was away visiting family one weekend. He went and got it from a scrap dealer, paid seven and sixpence for it and it was in pieces when he brought it home.

'If you want to ride that motorbike you fix it,' he said gesturing to the pile of pieces he'd laid out on the lawn.

He left me to get on with it and work it out myself. He was always there for support and advice but he knew the best way for me to learn was to let me make my own mistakes. It took me almost a year to rebuild it but eventually I turned the heap of rusting parts into a sparkling, pristine motorbike. Dad was not an emotional man but I like to think he was proud of me. I'm pretty sure he was. I loved that bike. It had two speeds – high and low – and it had an external brass flywheel that went off around your ankle. If you went up a hill you had to get off and push because it couldn't cope with gradients.

I stayed at school until I was eighteen. I dread to think how much my parents had invested in me by the time I left. The return on investment was ten O levels of varying grades. I studied for A levels but never completed the exams because, about two weeks before I was due to take them, I got my only bout of adolescent illness: I was hospitalized with appendicitis and had to have my appendix taken out.

Just before I left Freemen's we had a careers evening at school. Each pupil sat with a careers master and discussed their options. I had realized by then there was little chance of me becoming a vet. The master started the interview with the same questions he had asked the countless budding solicitors, bankers and clinicians he'd seen before me.

'So, what do you think you might want to do with yourself, Master Cowell?'

At the time the first James Bond movies had come out and I loved the action.

'W-well, I was thinking maybe a s-stuntman,' I stuttered.

The British movie industry was in its ascendancy and I figured it was the right time to launch myself into that career. The adviser looked at me like I had a brain that didn't work.

'A m-m-musician,' I shrugged.

'You might want to reconsider your options, young man,' he said.

CHAPTER TWO

Down on the Farm

WHAT THE . . . !'
I felt the back of the vehicle skid down the embankment and heard the snapping of hedgerow.

The inevitable tirade followed.

'Simon, you prat, how the hell are we are going pull it out of the ditch now?'

I knew one end of a cow from another but my tractor-driving skills left a lot to be desired. Sadly, the one thing I excelled at was tipping them into ditches, which always meant that the poor sod I was with would have to go back to the farm and bring out a Land Rover or another tractor to free the vehicle I had crashed.

My friend and long-suffering workmate in that incident and all the others which involved tractors and ditches was my cousin's husband, John Perkin, whose farm I washed up at after leaving school. I was in the Wild West (Devon to be precise) where I was getting my first taste of full-time work and I ended up there because I didn't have a plan – it just sort of happened, like so much else that followed in my life.

After my dreams had been cruelly crushed by the careers master at Freemen's, I fretted over my options. Stuntman was out, musician was unrealistic, vet was academically unlikely and so, with no options that were immediately compelling, I fell back on something that I already knew plenty about and decided to pursue a career in farming. I set my sights on a future farm-manager role and I got into Seale-Hayne College, which was an agricultural college in Devon. Rather than start straight away, I was advised that I would benefit from some work experience and so I deferred the placement for a year and arranged to work with John on his farm, which meant leaving home and going to live on the Devon and Cornwall border in a village called St Giles-on-the-Heath. My work covered my food and board and any money left over was mine.

I had the freedom of a car by then, having passed my test on my seventeenth birthday. My very first car was a second-hand 100E Anglia. I was always expected to buy my cars and pay for their running costs myself, and I bought my first from a friend of Dad. I kept blowing the gearbox up on it because it only had three speeds and not enough oomph to cope with my style of driving, which was foot-to-the-floor and has remained that way for most of my life. On regular weekends my little Anglia would end up in the workshop at Dad's work while the mechanics fixed it because I had blown up yet another engine. When that Anglia finally gave up the ghost within a year of me buying it, I traded up and got a 105E Anglia, which got me down to the Devon and Cornwall border in about four-and-a-half hours. The poor thing was always at the end of its rev limit.

John had a dairy herd, some sheep and some arable land. It wasn't a big farm and it wasn't particularly profitable. Given the amount of graft that it took to keep it running, I soon began to see that, from a business perspective, the fields of agricultural Britain were not sown with gold. Farming only really paid for people in the higher echelons – the landowners.

I liked being with the animals, however, and was not scared or nervous when called upon to get in the barn and muck out the cows. They didn't take much notice of me and just moved out the way with a shove when I needed to pass. I learned that as long as you avoided their horns, they were peaceful, benevolent creatures. I also liked the farming people. They were fun and foul-mouthed. They worked hard and played hard and I found a social circle there that I felt comfortable with. My stutter was rarely mentioned and, because farmers are not known for their eloquence, I didn't feel pressured or nervous when I spoke.

Soon after I moved to Devon I was taken out and introduced to one of the quaint local customs: getting trolleyed on scrumpy. I was not a big drinker or a regular pub-goer and the first time I got properly hammered was on a school-arranged outing to a musical. I was in the sixth form doing my A levels and my trumpet master at the time,

Frank Jones, who was a really nice guy, invited me to sit in on a show he was playing at in London.

'Come along, sit next to me in the orchestra and see how it all happens,' he said. He knew I loved musical theatre and had ambitions to be a musician and he thought it would be a good opportunity for me.

The musical was *The Man from La Mancha* and as we were behind the stage I didn't have to dress up. Frank was playing the overture and I watched the trumpet part – it was all quite interesting. At the end of the overture a big number seven appeared on a screen above the musicians, at which point they all got up and silently slunk out. Puzzled, I followed them and twigged what was going on. The screen indicated that they had seven minutes until the next number and in that time they sneaked into the bar next door and downed a drink. Wanting to fit in, I ordered myself a barley wine and knocked it back with them. Which was all fine until I got about halfway through part two. I wasn't used to drinking and felt the effects. I lost count at fourteen glasses and do not remember much about the finale or the journey home. Luckily it has always been my blessing to pass out when drunk before I am sick. My body closes down and allows me the dignity of a graceful coma, rather than the humiliation of throwing up.

My introduction to scrumpy was another baptism of boozy fire. John and I sat in the pub and he insisted the pints kept coming. Cider wasn't my thing and neither were pints but peer pressure prevailed and I managed to keep up, the youth of my liver giving me a competitive advantage over some of the yellowed, sclerotic farmhands we were drinking with. When the landlord declared that there was lock-in I remained resolute and continued knocking back the drink. It must have been something to do with the unique scrumpy effect but I didn't realize just how drunk I was getting until it was time to go home.

'I can't move my legs,' I said as I grabbed the edge of the table and tried to stand.

'C'mon, Simon, don't be an arse. It's two in the morning and you've got to get up at five to do the milking,' John slurred.

'But I can't move,' I mumbled.

John had to hoist me to my feet. Oddly, I felt sober as a judge and couldn't work out why my limbs didn't work. One of the soberer farmhands delivered us home and, once in my room, I passed out and dreamed of apples.

In addition to cider, I was introduced to another country pursuit during my tenure on the farm. I learned how to use a shotgun. Given my choice of vocation people are often surprised to hear that in my former life, before I started saving wildlife, I killed it. It is not something of which I am proud and it is not something I would condone or partake in today but I still have no problem with someone who shoots to eat. I eat meat and I enjoy eating meat. Humans are omnivores. We have evolved to be meat eaters and it seems logical to me that if you choose to eat meat you should not be squeamish about the fact that your choice ultimately means that something has died. You want dinner, you go out and shoot something, skin it and eat it. That, to me, is better than going to a supermarket and spending a few pounds on a chicken that has lived a short and miserable life and died in a very unpleasant way. The mechanization and industrialization of meat production are something I find abhorrent; everything is so intensive and unfair on the animal, which becomes a commodity, and a cheap one at that. I always buy organic and free range where I can and I think it takes guts to do the raising, killing and the preparation yourself. It's fairer and it makes you consider the impact of your diet choices. Even when you know it has had a good life I think it is still hard to turn an animal you have cared for into a casserole. I couldn't go out in the yard thinking, *I want chicken tonight. I'll have that one. I'll have Beatrice.*

Shooting on the farm was practical. Sometimes I would take a rabbit or pigeon for the pot, other times the shooting would be for pest control. I didn't delight in it but if a fox was taking chickens it was necessary. All the farmers had the same approach. If you needed to kill something you did it, quickly and efficiently.

I worked on the farm through the winter, braving the wet weather and taking delight in throwing my heroic Anglia around the country lanes. There wasn't a great deal to do other than drink and work so I entertained myself with country drives and attracted a bit of a name for myself as a boy racer. I don't know what possessed me – I just loved the adrenaline kick. The deserted, winding lanes lent themselves to my favourite style of driving (fast) and I became competent at negotiating the challenging twists and turns.

By the time spring arrived I had begun to question whether farming was really what I was destined to do. I wanted to enjoy life and I wondered whether I would enjoy a life of farming. I explained this to Dad, who could see that I wasn't 100 per cent sold on agriculture and one day, out of the blue, he called with an offer. Through the course of his work he had got to know a senior partner at a City of London brokerage firm called ED&F Man. The chap owned a farm and Dad had mentioned that he had a son who was coming up to his nineteenth birthday and who was at a loss as to what to do with his life.

'Tell him to come in for an interview,' the chap said. So I did.

I did not know the first thing about finance, markets, the City or stocks and shares but I was confident enough in my ability to learn quickly and, given the choice between a life of mud and cows in the west and the possibility of a decent wage and a warm office in the City, I didn't take much persuading. I explained the situation to John, who knew in a few months I would be off to college anyway and he encouraged me to give it a go. I drove up to Brockham at the weekend with my only suit in the back of the car. On the Monday morning I brushed the straw off it and, still smelling of cows, got on the train at Dorking with the rest of the commuters and headed to Mincing Lane where the firm had its headquarters.

ED&F Man was one of the City's historic businesses. It was initially founded as a sugar brokerage by businessman and trader James Man in 1783 and in the following year won the contract to supply the Royal Navy with rum for its sailors, each of whom were allocated a rationed daily shot – or tot as it was called. The tradition continued until 1970, two years before I went for my interview, and the company had expanded from sugar and rum into other commodities such as coffee and cocoa.

In truth, it was a scoop for me to get the interview. The City in those days employed a lot of ex-Army people and you were only likely to get in if you knew someone. It was a club and quite an exclusive one at that. Not knowing how fortunate I was worked in my favour. Having been on a farm for a year, people didn't tend to scare me or make me nervous. I walked into the ostentatious reception of the building, gave my name and sat on the leather sofa waiting to be called.

I was shown upstairs into a plush, wood-panelled boardroom. Seven men in suits were sitting around one end of a large oval table. I said hello and one of them gestured for me to sit in a single chair placed at the other end of the table. They were all very smartly dressed and, although I didn't know much about clothes, I could tell their suits were expensive. I became acutely aware of the bovine scent that was rising from my scratchy brown blazer. The men started firing questions at me left right and centre. It was a barrage.

'Tell us a bit about yourself.'

'What do you know about commodities markets?'

'What strengths could you bring to the job?'

'What's that smell?'

I tried to keep up with the questions but, after a minute or so, I held my hand up.

'Please, gentlemen,' I said. 'It's no good all asking at once. I can't answer you all at the same time. One at a time is fine.'

I saw a few of them exchange glances. The tempo of the interview slowed and we discussed my achievements – which I embellished somewhat. I told them about my exam results, my musical interests and that I enjoyed driving. I explained that I was used to hard work, enjoyed a challenge and was a fast learner and a problem solver. My stutter didn't run away with me and I talked slowly and purposefully. They explained that the job on offer was a commodities broker in sugar. I had no idea what that meant but it sounded interesting. I explained that my time spent on the farm had taught me about how commodities markets worked and how raw materials and food were traded.

After around thirty minutes they sent me out the room for a while and then called me back in.

'We are pleased to be able to offer you the job. When can you start?' the senior partner asked.

'Straight away,' I answered.

And that's how simple it was. I called John up and told him I wouldn't be back. He understood. I moved back in with my parents temporarily but a few weeks later bought my first property: a flat in Sutton, which cost £13,000. I started my City career on £800 a year plus bonuses, which was a decent wage in those days. I joined the rat race the day I turned nineteen; I bought a rail season ticket, a new suit (but not a bowler hat) and walked across London Bridge every working day for nearly twenty-three years. Initially, it was a massive culture shock but the money focused my mind and once I got in there I realized that money was actually quite nice to have and I started to enjoy the lifestyle it afforded me. Eventually, of course, it eats into your soul but we will come to that later. For the time being, I played the part of City trader and learned about commodities. There is a physical side – growing it, moving it, refining it – and there is the paper side – selling it and trading it. ED&F Man had 700 employees at the time and traded in huge quantities of goods. I soon realized why I got the job. The pace was frenetic and relentless, the office was busy and noisy. I had to juggle lots of things at once and they were looking for someone who stayed calm and focused under pressure, which I did in the interview.

I sailed through the first years as the firm expanded. I started trading with other countries. I sold sugar to Iceland or Israel. Then I got moved on to the futures department and the baying market floor with the screaming and the shouting. I loved the life. I had £50 notes in my pocket. I had money to burn. As a child every penny had been accounted for in the household. In my early twenties I had wealth I never dreamed of. I got used to it. I was a Master of the Universe. The farm in Devon and the unclaimed place at the agricultural college was a different life away.

CHAPTER THREE

International Playboy

THERE WAS A rigid hierarchy in the firm and everyone knew their place. I was at the bottom. At the pinnacle were the partners, to whom I looked up and who also scared the living daylights out of me. One of the bosses was a chap who could be lovely one day and not so lovely the next. I quickly learned to watch him from afar for a few minutes in the mornings to work out what sort of mood he was in. Once I'd gauged whether he was having a good day or a bad day I knew what I could and couldn't say and what I could get away with. Another of the partners was an Eastern European guy called Charles who did extremely well and made the company millions. He was a much more stable character and would often give me advice, which was generally 'keep your head down and do your job'.

It was a very noisy environment. There was plenty of shouting and chest-beating, especially on the trading floor which was housed in a place called Plantation House just across the road from our office. The trading floors were where traders went to buy and sell. Plantation House had different floors for different commodities – there was a coffee floor, a sugar floor, a cocoa floor and a spice floor. Around the edge of each there were lots of little telephone booths and, in those days, when someone took an order it was written on a greyscale screen with an electric pencil and the details then came up at the other end in the office. It was cutting-edge technology long before the days of computers.

At ED&F Man we traded physical sugar. A customer would ring me up from somewhere in the world and say that they wanted 5,000 tonnes of refined sugar of a certain quality. I would ring up someone who supplied it, be it Tate & Lyle or a refinery in Czechoslovakia, and match the seller and the buyer while taking a couple of dollars' commission from the deal. I'd arrange the shipping, the letters of credit and all the paperwork. The idea was to make a profit for the broker in the middle. So if Israel wanted to buy sugar for a certain price and someone was selling at a lower price the difference between the two was mine.

A few years after I joined the firm, it executed one of the most daring deals in sugar history. Sugar traders still talk about it with reverence today. The deal took Man from being a mid-sized brokerage to a huge one and involved shady Russian businessmen, diamonds, a glamorous Russian woman and lots and lots of sugar.

It was the middle of the Cold War and the USSR and the West were threatening each other with nuclear Armageddon.

Leonid Brezhnev was the communist leader and had overseen a huge expansion of the Soviet military during his tenure. Politically, the situation was tense. However, what much of the world didn't realize was that behind the politics, in the world of business, the communist Soviet Union was as much involved in the international markets as anyone else. Russians still needed coffee, spices, wheat and everything else. Soviet agriculture, with its centralized farms and government-imposed quotas, could not supply demand and Brezhnev's predecessor, Nikita Khrushchev, had started to import cereal, often from the mortal enemy, the USA. When Brezhnev had difficulties sealing commercial trade agreements with the United States, he went elsewhere to countries such as Argentina to do business. Another crop that started to hit the buffers in the USSR along with wheat was sugar beet. In the seventies, harvests declined by 2 per cent and subsequently the Soviets needed sugar from other sources.

They came to ED&F Man and the firm offered to help, knowing that when we started buying the huge quantities they needed, prices would rise considerably. At the time sugar was dirt cheap and the Soviets wanted to continue buying at that price. We bought up loads and sold it to them at the market rate and, as we did, the price rose, which meant we were taking a loss. However, very shrewdly and quietly we also went on the futures market and bought up huge amounts of paper sugar for a year or eighteen months forward. It was a long-game strategy. We lost money on the physical sugar that we sold at the cheap price but, as the prices rose and rose, the firm made a huge profit on the forward commodity they had bought. It was a huge deal worth millions and millions. The partners had to put up something called a performance bond to guarantee the fulfilment of the contract and, according to stories I heard, they all treble-mortgaged their houses to get the money together to fund the deal. There was huge risk involved but it paid off.

The deals also brought me and the rest of the sugar team into contact with a range of colourful characters from the East, not least a woman whom I'll call Madame G, who came over from Moscow to do the negotiating. The Cold War might have been getting frostier but you wouldn't have known it when the comrades from the Soviet sugar cooperative were in town. We were told to lavish gifts on them and spoil them rotten. Whatever they wanted they got and wherever they wanted to go they were taken. They came over with their bodyguards and stayed in suites at the Mayfair Hotel. If Madame G wanted a diamond ring she got a diamond ring. Hundreds of thousands of pounds were frittered away. It was how the world worked. It wasn't just the Soviets. If the deal was good enough no effort was spared. Once I remember walking across London Bridge with a briefcase full of krugerrands for a client because he had mentioned he wanted some. Gifts greased the wheels of commerce.

From day one I was earning more money than most of the people I knew who didn't work in the City. I replaced the Anglia with an MG Midget. My first bonus was a couple of hundred pounds and I bought my mum a bunch of flowers with it but it rose rapidly after that. A year later, in 1972, I was called in to receive my second bonus.

'Thank you for your work this year, Simon,' said the partner who handed me a folded up cheque. Politely I thanked him and put it in my pocket.

'Do you want to look at that?' he asked.

'No thank you, sir,' I said. I didn't want to appear rude.

'I think you might want to look at it,' he encouraged.

Very quickly I took it back out my pocket, unfolded it and glanced at it. I saw a number five. I assumed it was £500; twice my first bonus.

'Thank you very much, sir,' I said.

Later, when I looked at the cheque properly, I realized it was for £5,000, a huge sum of money for a twenty-one-year-old. Pretty soon after that I went into Reigate in Surrey and walked into a new car showroom. I looked over a brand new Triumph TR6 – a top-spec roadster – and as I did a pompous salesman came over and looked down his nose at me.

'Can I help you?' he sniffed.

'Just looking,' I said. I opened the door and got in. I heard him sigh so I looked over it a bit more. I started playing with the levers and the knobs on the dashboard. I could see him getting agitated. It was obvious he thought I was just messing around.

I got out of the car, stood back, tilted my head, looked at it and said absently: 'I think I'll take it.'

The salesman's tone changed in a microsecond. Suddenly, he couldn't be helpful enough. The car cost £1,908 and I still have the receipt. When I was presented with a company car – a Triumph Dolomite – my TR6 became the weekend run-around. I kept it for many years and sold it later for £3,500.

My social life started to revolve around work. Everyone went shooting and when I mentioned that I had an interest in the sport I got invited along, too. But after a while I became disillusioned. The shoots were just jollies for rich City folk. Herds of braying gents would go out and shoot hundreds of pheasants a day and I would sit back and think, *They are not going to get eaten, they are going to be buried in a hole in the ground*. It was during one of those business shoots that I put my sporting gun down for the last time. The shoots followed a pattern: pheasants in the day and duck in the evening. The ducks made easy targets in the twilight when they flew in to land and roost in reeds around the lake. With the weight of expectation on me I reluctantly shot one and it wheeled out of the sky, dead. Its mate circled in the red sky above it. I shot the mate and it died, too. I felt sick to my stomach. It was pointless. Two wasted lives. For what? For me and a load of rich toffs to boast to one another. I put my gun in its case.

'That's the last time I am ever going to shoot for the sake of shooting,' I said to no one in particular, and it was. It had screwed with my head and I couldn't handle it any more. I like to think that on that day I woke up. Shooting on that scale for those reasons turns the death of sentient beings into entertainment for other people. At least shooting pests on farms or rabbits for food had a purpose.

As I got busier I became a member of several London clubs and casinos. I was furnished with an unlimited expense account and a company American Express card, which was a status symbol. I was encouraged to entertain clients and there was no limit on what I could spend; the proviso I was told when the card was handed to me was to 'use it as necessary, providing you don't rip the arse out of it'. I was diligent and careful not to take liberties but when entertaining I spent what the client wanted me to spend. There was a lot of evening entertaining and a lot of expenses. I did what I had to do to make money for the company. Most days I was out to lunch in the City in a smart restaurant. In the evening I would be somewhere such as the Mayfair or the Ritz for dinner. I got a taste for fine dining. The clients then often wanted to go to a casino and gamble, and after that they sometimes wanted to go and do other more unmentionable things with ladies of the night. I provided it all.

Meanwhile, my parents were busy trying to fix me up with a wife to settle down with. Perhaps they watched from a distance and saw me getting increasingly seduced by the immoral lure of City life and wanted to anchor me to something more stable. They had long-term friends, originally from Gloucestershire, who had a daughter called Jill. Her father was a very well-to-do lawyer who worked for the Church and always wore a bowler hat. Jill and I had been introduced at a family event some years previously but hadn't quite hit it off. She was a very attractive girl but I was a bit of an arse at the time and I don't think she liked me very much. A few years later, however, we met again and I must have been on my best behaviour that time because we got on well. She was a musician and played the oboe and the clarinet. I still played the trumpet and so we had something in common. She had just finished studying at the Royal College of Music and was working for British American Tobacco in Westminster, next to the Houses of Parliament. As we were both young and worked in London, we arranged to meet up and started dating.

I'd had a few girlfriends before Jill but none of them were very serious. Despite the image I portrayed to the world – a young, confident, wealthy man-about-town – I was shy underneath the bravado and did not possess a great deal of self-confidence. I was still afflicted with a stutter and, consequently, I wasn't particularly good at chatting up women. But Jill was easygoing and fun to be with. She was a country girl at heart and we had a rural background in common. I enjoyed her company and, because our parents were friends, we shared a connection.

City life was becoming a drug. I was hooked on the money and spent all day on the phone, trading. During those first few years I never felt the pressure or stress. I liked the buzz and the adrenaline rush when I made a good trade and, unsurprisingly, I developed a taste for gambling. I couldn't really avoid casinos because many of my clients wanted to go to them after we had dined. One night I went with an Arab client and we played blackjack. I watch dumbfounded as he put down £1,000 chips, one after the other. He had piles of them stacked up in front of him and lost hand after hand.

He blew about £30,000 in five minutes and his expression didn't change. I remember thinking, *If he had given me half that money I would have been giggling for the rest of the evening*. It was a different world, far removed from the one I had grown up in and, at the time, I loved it. But unlike some of my gambling acquaintances I was cautious. I went with a set amount of money in my pocket: £50. If I lost it, I walked away; if I won, I walked away. I was always controlled. It took willpower not to get sucked in. I often placed 33–1 bets on roulette and won on several occasions. My favourite casino was the Hertford, which was just off Park Lane in Mayfair. As I was a frequent visitor, I was invited to their loyalty dinners which was quite cool because I could eat and drink a free meal with guys who were spending tens of thousands and it would only cost me my £50 stake money.

My relationship with Jill became more serious and she increasingly stayed over at my flat. Eventually I decided to ask her to marry me. We had talked about living together so marriage seemed like a natural progression. There was no big proposal: I asked and she agreed. My parents were away on holiday with friends so we waited until they came back before telling both sets of parents. They were all pleased for us but Jill's father was a little upset because I had not asked his permission first and, being a traditional kind of bloke, he thought things like that were important.

We married very soon after in June 1974 when I was twenty-two. Two days before the wedding I was in Paris at the annual sugar-traders evening, which was always held in the French capital and was the highlight of the calendar.

It was a lavish and exotic affair with lots of glamorous women, limitless booze and plenty of bad behaviour.

I returned to the UK with my morality intact and got married in a church in the Gloucestershire village where Jill had grown up. On the day all I could think about was how I was going to say my vows because I was terrified of having to speak in public. I managed to get through without a hitch and Jill and I settled down to married life. It was a lovely day and I even had my dog, a poodle named Rags, driven up from Surrey to be there.

In the year we married we moved from Sutton further out in the Surrey countryside to a village called Headley, where I had bought an old house. It had been built in 1510 and was a beautiful cottage, full of character. The boy's toys started fairly soon after that. After about three years of City life I decided to try my hand at rallying and built a car with a friend. We cut our teeth on Autocross, which is basically racing home-modified cars on fields. Racers compete against the clock on a closed, predefined circuit and, depending on the course, sometimes more than one car races at once, which increases the chances of contact. It is raw, muddy and great fun. We took turns driving. I got hooked and we soon progressed to Rallycross, which are sprint races held on closed, mixed-surface circuits with modified production or specially built road cars.

We bought a Hartwell Hillman Imp, which was small but went like a rocket, and at weekends were regulars at Lydden Hill circuit near Canterbury. Motorsport allowed me in indulge my passion for speed without the restriction of legally enforced regulations. I went for it and had no fear. I took a very nonchalant attitude to my own safety and indeed to the safety of those around me, often much to the chagrin of the poor soul who happened to be my co-driver. If I rolled it, I rolled it. In one of my first races I sat on the start line and revved, waiting for the green light. Adrenaline coursed through me. I'd driven the circuit previously and tried to memorize each turn and bump as best as I could. As the seconds until the start ticked down, the cockpit of the car began to fill with thick white smoke. The cars were inevitably works in progress. They broke down often, were patched up and held together with equal amounts of mechanic know-how and blind faith. Consequently, the sudden blanket of smoke did not concern me and I trusted that it would start to clear when I moved. I knew I had a hundred-metre straight dash and then I had to make a ninety-degree right turn. The klaxon sounded and the race was off. I put everything into it. I floored the accelerator and the engine screamed. More smoke belched into the cockpit. Guessing I'd cleared the straight I tugged the wheel into the turn as gradually the smoke cleared, at which point I realized I was still on the starting line and everyone else had left and was already a quarter of the way around the track. The clutch had burned out!

There were many mechanical failures and motorsport soon became an expensive hobby. The first car probably cost a couple of grand and in the end we would take a mechanic with us because we knew that on any given circuit we would go through at least four tyres and possibly some rims, and maybe something would break on the car. On plenty of occasions I would finish a stage with at least one or two tyres off and I'd be driving on the rims, sparks flying. There was no stopping to change the wheel: you got to the end in as best shape as you could and worried about the damage after. I would bend the car regularly, spinning off, hitting trees.

As we progressed to rallying proper, which takes place on public or private roads with modified production or specially built road-legal cars, the vehicles got more expensive and more powerful. I funded the rallying from my own pocket. It was my hobby and my release after a week spent in the pressure cooker of work. We bought a Vauxhall Chevette, which was modified and turned into a beast with twin Dellorto 48 carburettors on it, a limited slip diff and a five-speed straight-cut gearbox. The thing flew and the noise it made when it was opened up was unholy because all the acoustic muffling gear had been stripped out. It was so noisy when we were racing that we needed to wear helmets with built-in headphones and microphones to communicate. On the road, however, it looked and sounded fairly unassuming, apart from the low-profile tyres, the massive exhaust and the rally paintjob.

Eventually I worked out that it was cheaper for me to invest in a garage than to fund my hobby from my own pocket. I had enough spare money and wanted to put money into a business anyway, which would have the benefit of free mechanics who could do all the work on my cars. So, along with a business partner, I bought a mechanic's garage in Ashtead and we called it CWK Motors.

As the years rolled on rallying wasn't enough. I craved adrenaline so I started taking flying lessons and was hooked from the moment I clambered in a two-man single-engine starter plane. I learned quickly and I got on well with the other guys at the airport; there was the same kind of camaraderie and shared interest as there was in rallying, but with flying there was no competition against each other. We did it because we loved it. I loved the freedom of the open skies and the challenge of knowing that everything had to be done properly because the implications of getting something wrong were extremely serious. The process of learning to fly and getting a pilot's licence was great fun because my instructor and I would fly across to the Isle of Wight for lunch, have a few drinks and fly back. Regulations were much more lax then and I wouldn't be able to do that now. On one occasion my teacher got pissed at lunch and, as we were taking off from Bembridge Airport while I was at the controls, he thought it would be a good idea to open the door as a joke. I lost concentration momentarily and only just cleared the runway.

One summer, myself and two friends, one of whom was a pilot, hired a twin-prop plane and flew down to Le Mans in central France to watch some racing and then on to the South of France for a few days before coming back to Jersey and on to the UK. One morning we lost our pilot and eventually found him staying as a guest of the local Gendarmerie after a slight altercation during the previous night. We had to bail him out.

Flying scared me but I got a massive thrill from it as well.

The memory of my first solo flight will always stay with me. Take off was very busy – there was a lot to concentrate on, everything had to be done in order and precisely – so I didn't have time to worry. But then when I was up there at over 300 metres I suddenly panicked because there was no one there with me.

I got to my cruising height, did the first turn and then flew in a straight line for about five minutes. I suddenly wanted to cry because it was such a lonely feeling. All the self-doubt poured in and my mortality was brought into sharp focus. It was a huge eye opener and I struggled to keep my emotions and concentration in check. That, to me, was the biggest learning curve throughout my flight training. I wanted my first landing to be clean and as I came in after a single circuit I wasn't confident so I did what is called a touch and go. I touched the runway and took straight off again. I went up the second time and at that point was saying to myself, *Fuck! I can't land this thing, I am going to die.*

Despite the fear/healthy respect I continued to fly regularly for many years and went from fixed wing planes to helicopters because I liked the idea of being able to land anywhere. I only had about five lessons, though, because it was much more expensive. The first time I went up the instructor took the helicopter to about 3 metres above the runway and held the thing dead steady. Then he let me take the controls and we veered from side to side as I battled to steady the chopper. Next he took us up to about 300 metres.

'You've heard that if a helicopter engine dies you are dead, I assume?' he said.

I nodded.

Then he turned off the engine. I grabbed my seat momentarily as the cockpit went silent but rather than plummet from the sky the motion of the still turning rotors gave us enough lift to feather down and land safely. He explained that the only time you die when a helicopter engine cuts out is if something called the 'Jesus bolt' fails and the prop jams. As long as the blades turn the helicopter comes down at a controlled rate, which ironically was a fair analogy of my life at the time. My blades were turning. Work in the day, play at weekends. Late nights, casinos, cars, racing, planes and helicopters. It didn't even change when the children came along. I didn't notice the wear and tear on my psychological Jesus bolt!

CHAPTER FOUR

Answering a Call of Nature

I HAVE FOND MEMORIES of the house in Headley. It was warm and cosy and smelled comfortable and familiar in that way old buildings do. It had low, oak-beamed ceilings and anyone over 1.75 metres tall couldn't stand in the lounge without ducking between the beams. The house was set in an acre of land stocked with mature trees and we had a large lawn. After the warm, dry summer of 1975 I decided it would be a good idea to dig a swimming pool in the garden and employed a professional pool company to start work, which they did the following spring. Unfortunately, by the time they had excavated a decent-size hole in the garden, lined it properly and installed the plant that would keep the water filtered, the summer had developed into one of the hottest on record and the country was in full-scale drought. It was a nationwide emergency, which left me in a bit of a quandary. Water was being rationed, people were filling up jerry cans from standpipes and I needed almost 80,000 litres. Empty swimming pools have a habit of collapsing in on themselves – the pressure of the water keeps them rigid – which put me in the difficult position of having to make a rather embarrassing call to the water board.

'Hello. Look, I have a problem. I have a pool which is empty and it needs to be commissioned,' I explained apologetically. (Commissioning a pool means filling it up and finishing the job.)

'That's not ideal, sir,' I was told. 'But if it needs to be commissioned you'd better commission it. Just do it discreetly, please.'

And so very quietly I set about filling my pool with water, which took about a day and half. I really didn't have much choice at the time. When I think about that now, as a committed environmentalist, glugging thousands of litres of precious water into a pool in the middle of a drought seems ridiculous and, with the benefit of education, I certainly wouldn't do such a thing today. In my defence, climate change was not a concept the general public had any awareness of back then. We were all blissfully ignorant, living in a consumption-heavy bubble with no clue about the iceberg up ahead.

It was certainly a blessing to have the pool in the boiling summer. Jill used it regularly. I dipped in occasionally but, even though that summer broke all temperature records, the pool was never warm enough for me.

Life was good. I continued to earn what was by most standards a large salary and to the outside world I looked wealthy. I had a warped relationship with money. I was doing deals for millions of pounds and, when you deal with figures so mind-bogglingly large, money starts to lose its value. It was like playing Monopoly.

In all my time at ED&F Man the most I ever earned was a £50,000 basic annual salary and a quarterly bonus which was always roughly a quarter of my salary, so the total annual figure was around £100,000. That was in the nineties and was a decent wage, but other people were earning £1 million a year. I liked to think I could make money and seal deals but I never had the business acumen of some of my colleagues who earned bonuses ten or twenty times their salaries. They were the real big boys; the whizz kids who came to the office dressed in Savile Row suits and wearing Rolex watches. My brain never allowed me to be fast-tracked. You had to be very sharp to reach the same level as those people.

I was aware that my stutter held me back. It slowed me down because I had to concentrate harder on what I said. I took longer than others to get my words out and when I had to make split-second decisions and communicate what I wanted clearly yet urgently, my speech impediment would sometimes cost me valuable seconds. I was conscious of people looking at me and sometimes I couldn't make calls. I knew my bosses realized I had a problem but it was never mentioned. It was the elephant in the room.

Then one day it was finally addressed and miraculously that became a cathartic moment. I had been having a bad day and struggled through an important call. I can't remember the exact details but it would have been some sort of deal negotiation. The frustration of not being able to articulate what I needed to say fed the stutter and made it worse. It was a vicious circle: the more I tried, the worse the stutter became, and the worse it got, the more I had to try. One of my bosses was watching and after I hung up he walked over to me, put his hand on my shoulder and very quietly but firmly said: 'That's enough of the stuttering now, Simon.'

He patted me and walked away. I didn't show it but I was mortified. I didn't know what to do and I had no idea how to make myself stop. But, amazingly, within a few days I started to notice that speaking became easier. I was intensely aware of how my speech was coming out and made a huge effort to try and be clearer and more concise. Within a couple of weeks my stutter reduced to a tenth of what it had been. I haven't got a clue what happened but obviously some process in my brain changed, like a switch being flicked. My stutter was never mentioned again and from that day on speech was much easier. Today, sometimes the stutter comes back and I stumble, usually when I am stressed or nervous, but it has never reached the level it was when I was a young adult.

Losing it was a huge weight off my shoulders. My performance at work improved and I enjoyed the many opportunities for socializing even more. It is fair to say that I fully availed myself of all the opportunities and free meals and drinks that came my way.

Jill and I had an active social life with plenty of friends. She, I assumed, was happy. I went off most weekends and indulged myself in my money-burning hobbies. She worked and looked after the home. I was happy with my lot. I didn't have a five- or a ten-year plan. I never sat down and worked out a career path and I didn't have career ambitions other than the desire to make money. I went with the flow.

Soon after we got married Jill fell pregnant with our first daughter, Louisa. I had never planned parenthood either and when we did talk about family and children, I always approached the subject with the sort of attitude that you reserve for notional events that will probably happen at some point in the indeterminate future; it was an abstract concept. When Lou arrived I carried on as if nothing had happened. My life didn't alter. I am ashamed to say I took a back seat and let Jill get on with it. I was engrossed in my own world, working increasingly long and stressful hours and going off at weekends to do my own thing. I can't recall changing a nappy, I didn't do the feeds; my job was to earn the wage, which is not a fashionable view today but the early eighties were less enlightened times and I was not alone in being a largely absent, working father. That is not to say that I didn't appreciate what a very tough job child rearing was.

I started looking for a new house for us to live in. While the cottage was lovely and served our needs, it was small and I felt we needed somewhere bigger with a bit more land. Jill was not as enthusiastic as I was – she was happy where we were – but I went looking anyway and I found a place in Leatherhead that I persuaded her to view. It was an old farmhouse with outbuildings and plenty of land. It felt right as soon as I walked inside. Randalls Farm had a good energy and felt familiar, perhaps because I had grown up around farms. There was a coach house in the grounds where people travelling to London would have stopped over to rest and feed and water their horses in the old days. The stone trough for the horses was still outside. There were gardens and then land beyond on which there were a few buildings and a barn. The rest of the farmland that used to surround the house had been sold off and developed over the years but, while there were several business parks nearby, the area still felt like the countryside. Just over the road was Leatherhead Crematorium – so we knew the neighbours would be quiet – and the River Mole was a five-minute walk away. Jill liked it and, because it needed some work, it was on the market for a lot less than it was worth. I nearly bought it without telling Jill – I put in an offer and only told her afterwards. We paid £90,000 for it and at the time it was worth £120,000 so I was pleased with the deal.

A year after we moved Jill fell pregnant once more. Again, it just sort of happened and Jill didn't even tell me the news first: she told my parents. I found out by surprise on a trip to Gloucestershire. We were driving there to visit her parents and my folks were in the car with us looking after Lou when Mum mentioned it. Jill probably didn't want to bother me, given the amount of time I'd spent with Lou.

Of course, I was delighted and Gemma came along several months later. Randalls Farm became a proper home. We had our own family unit. With two young mouths to feed I found myself working even harder and longer hours, and Jill still looked after the children without any assistance from me. I was a spectator and I regret not seeing the kids as much as I should have when they were little. There is a big hole that I can't ever fill. In retrospect I was an awful father who was never there and I will feel guilty about that until the day I die.

Jill never complained. She got on with the job of raising our daughters and I get so cross now when I hear people use the phrase 'only a housewife' because it is obvious to me that it is bloody hard work.

Several life-changing things happened in the year after we moved. In addition to Gemma's birth we had another new arrival, which consequently would change the course of all of our lives. Jill and I had always kept pets. We had a golden retriever named Max who moved with us to Randalls Farm. There was plenty of space for him to roam around in and plenty of space for anything else. We were both animal lovers and we also both harboured unfulfilled ambitions to work with animals in some capacity or another. We had both wanted to be vets when we were younger but lacked the required qualifications. Then one day we got a call from an old friend of ours asking a favour. And she had a box with her.

It was Anne Cooper, the slightly eccentric wildlife rescuer and former neighbour from Brockham. She explained the purpose of her visit. We were both equally bemused and flummoxed.

'I've got a neighbour. She had a seagull in her flat. It only has one wing . . .'

'What are you talking about, Anne?' I interrupted.

'Here,' she said, opening the box and showing me the grumpy-looking bird.

'The poor thing couldn't stay where it was. It was living in a bath. Your mum told me there is a bit of space at your new place. I thought perhaps you could give it a home?'

Jill and I looked at each other.

'Why not?' we said.

Anne was part of a network of people that helped the local wildlife and they all seemed to know each other and swapped tips and advice. If one had an animal that couldn't go back in the wild for whatever reason, they would ask around in the community and try to find a home for it if they couldn't keep it themselves. It was a bonkers little world, but extremely good-natured and quite noble. These people had their own reasons for doing what they did – I thought that some of them were just lonely while others were a bit dotty – but ultimately they were doing good things and helping animals.

I took the box from Anne and she explained the basics of caring for the gull. Luckily gulls eat almost anything so there was no problem sourcing food for it.

'It's all right,' I said soothingly to the animal, 'we are not going to hurt you. Welcome to your new home.'

The bird was quite used to being handled and let me pick him up.

'He's very gentle,' Anne said. 'His beak isn't that sharp and I should imagine he will be okay with the children.'

'Patient zero' made itself at home inside and outside the house. It would waddle in the kitchen looking for scraps. I had always planned on building a pond so we dug one out soon after the gull arrived. The bird loved it and a few months later it had company. My dad had a new job managing a farm for a friend and he decided to sell the family home and move into a cottage on the farm. The house Dad was selling had a pond, which was home to a swan. The swan had just appeared in his yard one day and wasn't very well. Dad fed it and looked after it and it became part of the family. He was devastated when he thought he was going to have to rehome it somewhere new. He was happy to let us have it, and he could visit it anytime he liked.

That is how all it began, with a seagull in a bath tub and a swan. Word spread that we took in animals and every now and then someone would call and explain that they had found something in their garden or something injured by the roadside and they brought it to us. I had enough knowledge from my farming days to know the rudimentary stuff when it came to animal first aid. Jill was more than capable and learned quickly. She loved having animals to look after. Our animal centre began to grow organically without us advertising or announcing it. It was pure word of mouth. It just happened and we did it because we enjoyed it. It was a hobby. I came home from work and looked after a few things. It was relaxing and a diversion from the stress of the City. I seemed to know what I was doing and had a natural affinity with the animals. When we'd patched our patients up we released them back into the wild. If they couldn't go back, we found homes for them on the farm. We called ourselves Randalls Wildlife Rehabilitation Centre.

CHAPTER FIVE

Animal House

AS IT HAPPENED, Dad didn't have to wait long to be reunited with his swan because a few years later he and Mum moved into our coach house, which had been hastily converted into a cosy bungalow. They brought along a few other additions of their own. Sadly, Dad's fortunes had not worked out as well as he deserved or expected. The job on the farm was brought to a swift conclusion after a dispute with the farm owner. When Dad had sold the family home to move into the farm he had let it go too cheaply – I think he got around £30,000, which, for a four-bedroom detached house, was well below what it was worth at the time. Dad had worked hard all his life and ultimately had little to show for it when the farm job came to an end. With limited savings my parents were effectively homeless. Jill and I invited them to come and live with us at Randalls. Dad was such a kind, decent bloke who always had time for everyone that it didn't need any further consideration. I was never going to allow my parents to be without a home; they had made so many sacrifices for me when I was growing up and, as far as I was concerned, it was an opportunity to pay them back – not that they expected it. So they arrived with their 'family'. Dad had been collecting a small menagerie of water fowl, which he transferred to our pond. The seagull looked slightly disgruntled at having to share his home with a load of new arrivals.

Throughout my life, circumstance has always provided in some way or another at crucial times; call it fate or divine intervention. That is what happened when my parents arrived. Dad was a brilliant handyman who could fix anything. He never needed to be asked – he just enjoyed the simple pleasure of finding something that was broken or could be improved in some way and tinkering with it. Consequently, within a few months of his arrival there was nothing on the farm that didn't work. If something broke it was fixed within a day. I would walk through the garden, notice the outside tap was leaking and make a mental note to fix it, but by the next day it was already done. It was like having a magical elf who invisibly mended things. He went about the place very quietly and unassumingly, and was always there in the background. Everyone loved him to bits and he was a true gentleman. He also loved wildlife and knew several people from his farming network who soon got to know about our willingness to take in wildlife. Our 'hobby' quite quickly turned into something much more. We never dreamed it would be anything more than a pastime and we never really meant for it to expand. Initially our patients found a home in the kitchen.

We didn't advertise but the community was closer than it is today and people talked. Subsequently, every so often someone would arrive with a box. The exchange was always the same. There would be a knock on the door, usually at the weekend or in the evening. Jill or I would get up and open it.

'Hello. A friend told me that you look after wildlife and I found this,' they would say, offering the box for inspection. They would be invited inside.

'What have you got there then?' I would enquire curiously.

The lid would be lifted and something would be nestling inside in some straw or ripped newspaper, rustling around nervously.

I would then start asking questions to get as much information as I could about the creature – what injuries it had and where it had been found. I would take down the patient's details on a pad that Jill helpfully left out by the door, attached to the wall with a piece of string. It was our log and helped us keep track of things. It was inevitable that I would take in the animal with the aim of feeding it, treating any injuries and ultimately getting it back out into the wild. Most commonly in the early days we would get small birds and hedgehogs. The hedgehogs were magical and we would be constantly rearranging our kitchen to cope with the growing number. We certainly didn't go into it thinking we were going to create a wildlife hospital in our home. I can't really blame anyone else because I let it grow and grow and tacitly encouraged it with a call to the local newspaper or the local radio station here and there, explaining that a new visitor had arrived. The local press loved it because there is nothing more heart-warming for the readers than a picture of a little baby hedgehog. After each small snippet in the papers we received more animals.

We had cages to keep the animals in and we utilized household goods to deal with emergencies as and when they arose. It was think-on-your-feet firefighting. One day a woman arrived with a box and showed me a fully intact nest in which sat several tiny birds cheeping weakly. They were so fragile and young their featherless skin was translucent and their closed eyes bulged like black wounds.

'A cat got their mother and the father never came back,' the woman said. 'I got my husband to get up the tree on the ladders and get the nest. I couldn't stand there and do nothing. I could hear them calling for their mother. It was awful.'

I reassured the woman and told her we would do our best to get them fit and healthy, and big enough to fend for themselves back in the wild.

'Thank you so much,' she said. She was genuinely emotional.

'You've done the right thing,' I told her. Naively I believed back then that human intervention was predominantly the best course of action. Over the years I learned that was a false assumption and often, especially with baby birds, the best thing to do if they are not in immediate peril is to do nothing as one or both parents will usually return. Even birds that fall from the nest often find their way to a safe hiding place where a parent will continue to feed them.

When the woman left I started to think about the challenge I had just accepted. I had a nest full of birds that needed to be fed and kept warm. I racked my brains to think of where to put them. Eureka! We had an electric frying pan – one of those gadgets that you buy because they seem like a good, time-saving idea but that you never use. I dragged it out from the back of the cupboard, cleared space on a worktop, put it on the lowest setting and placed the nest gently on it. Then I grabbed my coat and car keys and went to a local angling shop to buy a pint of maggots. Back at home I found a bowl and mashed up some of the maggots into a smelly, revolting paste and, using a turkey baster, I spent the next thirty minutes feeding the birds. They loved it and over the following weeks we made several trips to the angling shop to keep a constant supply of mashed maggots, which the birds devoured hungrily. Thankfully, Jill and I had grown up in rural communities so we were not precious about the kitchen and keeping it spotless. Farmhouse kitchens are always in a state of organized chaos, with people and dogs traipsing in and out. Ours was the same, full of life and wildlife. The gas-fired Aga was regularly used to warm a patient. We patched up animals, bathed wounds and disinfected them.

'Remember the oven when you go, there is a hedgehog in there,' Jill would call out as I ventured off to work. She would prepare breakfast for the girls, then start to feed the animals. I got as involved as I could during the weekends and the evenings, but Jill did all the hard work.

It was a steep learning curve to begin with as there was no internet from which to get information. If only we had Google back then, it would have made life a hell of a lot easier. There was much trial and error and I utilized the network of other animal carers who were doing similar things. We shared information. Anne Cooper was a constant source of support and advice and if she didn't know something she would be able to put me in touch with someone who did. I made telephone calls to the RSPCA and to other wildlife rescue centres, the most established of which was called Tiggywinkles, based in Buckinghamshire. It had been set up by a man called Les Stocker and his wife Sue in 1978, two years before we started our little enterprise. I saw Les on the news and it inspired me to some extent. I thought, *If they can do it, we can.*

Slowly, as we became more established, people started calling us for advice, too. The guiding purpose of what we did was to get injured animals back into their natural habitats but on occasion things would arrive at our door that were too damaged to survive in the wild or which had been kept as pets and were too imprinted by man. That, to me, is the worst-case scenario for any animal. It has lost its natural survival instinct and instead is a prisoner to man. As the years went on I formulated a strict philosophy, which I'll explain later. However, in our early years we took in several animals that became permanent fixtures in and around the house. One of the first was Fleur, a beautiful barn owl.

At this point it is important to explain a little about my thoughts on naming animals. I believe that anthropomorphizing wild animals – attributing human characteristics to them – is the first step to imprinting them. Wild animals don't have names because they are not pets, so I have tried to make a policy over the years of never naming things when they are brought in. My policy works sometimes but other times my daughters or, in later years, volunteers would give something a name. Fleur, however, already had a name when she arrived. She was delivered by the RSPCA. I had become friendly with one of the local inspectors, a very lovely man named Bill Alston.

Bill called me one day and explained that he had confiscated an owl from a person in Surrey because the bird was being mistreated and was being kept in a cage. He asked if I had room for her. We had the barn at the top of the farm, which could easily be sectioned up to create a secure aviary space, so I agreed straight away. Owls are magnificent, intriguing creatures and this one deserved a better life. Dad set about making a suitable enclosure and Bill brought Fleur over. It was evident from the very start that she had no fear of humans, which is not a good thing for a wild animal. Bill explained the dos and don'ts of owl care and left Fleur with us. She made herself right at home and hopped onto my shoulder while I held the tether attached to her leg. She surveyed the chaos of the kitchen, twisting her head from side to side, making a careful note of the animals in cages arranged around the room, no doubt thinking what tasty snacks they would make. I made a note to keep her well-fed in case she was ever tempted to help herself to one of the patients. Dead chicks were added to the weekly shopping list that included maggots, earthworms, dog food, cat food and sprats for the seagull.

People started to call when they saw stranded wildlife and sometimes I would go and collect animals if I was around. From there the rescue service began. The very first rescue happened soon after we started out. It was Sunday and the phone rang. I answered and spoke to the manager of a local golf course.

'We have a problem with a swan on the eighteenth tee,' he explained. 'The blasted thing has been there for hours and it won't move. If you approach it, it hisses and no one wants to get attacked. It's holding up all the members – they can't play through.'

'Is it injured at all?' I asked.

'We've not been able to get close enough but it certainly isn't moving,' he explained.

'I'll be right over,' I said.

I went out to the garage and started to rummage around for any equipment I might need. I grabbed a pole, reasoning that from a distance I would be able to gently nudge the swan to see if it could be moved. I took a large fishing net in case I needed to try and catch it and I took the biggest carry-cage we had. I also took a pair of thick leather gloves. I packed it all up in the boot of the car and drove to the course where I was met by the exasperated manager, his face red with frustration at the obstinate swan that was ruining Sunday for his members. He showed me across the green to the scene of the crime.

The tee was surrounded by members, mostly men in various shades of pastel all looking equally irritated. The manager pointed.

'There it is,' he said, with barely concealed ire.

I looked over to where he was gesticulating and there, sitting on the immaculate grass, was a rather magnificent male adult swan looking totally unfazed by the commotion around it.

'Leave it to me,' I said confidently, while thinking, *Okay, what am I going to do now?*

Slowly and deliberately I walked towards the swan. I glanced at it but I didn't look it directly in the eyes. I sensed that would only aggravate it and I didn't want to appear threatening. Having been around animals all my life I had an innate sensitivity to them: I could read their moods and body language and I could tell the swan wasn't distressed. It seemed quite calm. I got the distinct impression it was just being obstinate and awkward. I was used to Dad's swan so I had a good idea of the type of temperament they had and this one was displaying typical swan arrogance. I also knew that while you have to respect them, the adage that a swan can break a leg with a wing is a myth, unless you suffer from something like brittle bone disease. I also knew that, on the whole, swans were all bark and no bite. Almost on cue, as I neared the subject of my first rescue it reared up, spread its wings and started hissing.

I could hear some mumbling from the golfers who were

now enthralled, probably hoping that I would be attacked.

'Don't be so silly,' I said quietly but firmly and carried on walking slowly towards the bird, which started to beat its wings, roll its eyes and honk. I knew I couldn't back down. For one, I needed to show the swan that I wasn't scared, but mainly I didn't want to look like an idiot in front of my audience.

As I got to within a few steps of the bird it stopped making a fuss, and slumped back down again with a dejected look on its face.

'Good swan,' I said. I stepped forward, reached out slowly and got hold of it. It made an indignant grunt but allowed itself to be handled. I took care not to hurt it but made sure I held it firmly enough around its wings so it couldn't start flapping around. I also held it far enough from me facing away so it couldn't turn round and peck me. Then I walked back towards the manager.

'Where do you want it?' I called.

'Can you take it back to the lake on the twelfth, please?' he said.

I walked past the golfers and released the swan back to where he should have been. It let me carry it all the way without a fuss.

A successful rescue release, where the animal went straight back in the wild without needing to stay at the farm, was the gold standard for the animal and for us because we were being overrun. Each morning the girls sat at the table having breakfast before going off school, oblivious to the activity around them. They knew nothing else. They couldn't understand why there was always a long line of school friends waiting to be invited back to the house for tea. When they were young their birthday parties must have been the most eagerly awaited in the school. Kids loved the house because there was always something exciting to see there. Fleur added to the lure of it all because, although she had a home in the barn, she spent a lot of time in the house. In the end she lived with us for twenty years – in the wild, barn owls live for around six. She became an unofficial mascot and would come to fundraising events with me and to the school talks I later gave. In hindsight I feel sorry for her because it must have been a crappy life for a wild animal. If I had known more when we first took her in I would have tried to get her back into the wild. She might not have lived long but the quality of her life would have been far better.

If I was presented with the same situation today I would act differently. We didn't put things to sleep that perhaps we should have done back then. A lot of people will find that difficult to understand because they believe that by keeping a wild animal captive, you are helping it. In my opinion you are not – you are torturing it. People still do it today – they put a crow in a cage because it only has one wing. That's like you or I living the rest of our lives in a telephone box. It is not fair. We should have respect for wildlife: it should be flying freely or running around in the wild and should enjoy its life. I think if it doesn't have that sort of life it shouldn't be here. I learned these things as I went along but it took many years and, at the beginning, all I could do was follow my heart and feelings.

Another permanent resident arrived soon after Fleur. It was a mentally impaired deer. We never found out its story and without an MRI scan we had no idea what was really wrong with it apart from the fact that you could tell just by looking at it that it wasn't in possession of all its faculties. It had lost its marbles. We made an enclosure for it and kept it in the garden for years. It was skittish and nervous, would fit occasionally and wasn't particularly confident on its feet. Dad was the only one who could get close to it. He had a way with animals, which is probably where I got it from. He loved that deer, even after it stuck its antler right through his leg one day.

Meanwhile, the dogs remained calm and took the presence of all the other animals for granted, which was bizarre because out on a walk they would chase anything. But if they were walking up the garden and a duck waddled across the lawn they totally ignored it.

For several years I funded the project personally with the money I was making in the City. I hate to think what I spent on it in all – probably somewhere between £100,000 and £200,000. I bought equipment, food, medical supplies and bedding. We begged and borrowed as well. We spoke to local hospitals and got the dressings and ointments that they threw away. We also began approaching vet practices and often, when we had an animal which we couldn't patch up ourselves, they would help out with stitches or antibiotics. We received great support from a local vet who came on board and volunteered her time early on. Her name was Joyce Tibbetts and she was wonderful. She did brilliant work for us for many years. Joyce would come in and perform procedures if we needed her. Often vets would call us after people had taken injured wildlife to them and they had patched the animals up and needed someone to care for them as they recovered.

When the children went to school Jill's days were consumed with looking after all the animals, feeding them, cleaning them, caring for them and medicating them. By the late 1980s the trickle had become a flow. We grew naturally, which was good in retrospect because it allowed us to learn as we went along. On the 7.03 from Leatherhead to Waterloo I was the only City gent reading wildlife and veterinary manuals, rather than *The Times* or the *Daily Mail*. Later, I developed an idea for a storybook for children about a one-eyed owl that found itself injured in a rescue centre. While others gazed out of the train window on their journeys to work, I sat huddled over a pad scribbling away intently for many months, writing down the story which was eventually published as *The Owl with the Golden Heart*. I'm still immensely proud of the book today.

When it became too busy for Jill to cope on her own we started to ask for volunteers, firstly among friends and neighbours. One lady came in and said she wanted to help on one afternoon a fortnight. She ended up being our most senior volunteer and she was amazing; she did everything Jill did, and which a veterinary nurse does now. Sadly, she died of cancer several years ago. We found that people were willing to come in and help, which was a bonus because we could not pay for staff. As the overall costs rose, I could no longer afford to keep up so we started tentatively fundraising. We would ask people who brought in patients for donations and on the whole they were happy to leave a few pounds in the knowledge that we would do our best to look after whatever it was they had saved.

In 1987 we became a registered charity and renamed ourselves Wildlife Aid. It was easier to ask for money as a charity. I was still working and I never hid what I was doing from my bosses. I'm sure they didn't like it and most of my colleagues probably thought I was slightly mad. I got reprimanded now and then for calling on the work phone to check on a patient's progress and, if truth be told, I was often preoccupied with things back on the farm more than I was at work. In 1992 we opened a surgery, which we created in a room at the front of the house, and the singer Beverley Craven came and opened it. It was a fully functioning veterinary surgery with equipment bought by funds we had collected or which had been donated by businesses. It was a far cry from the first medical shed I had erected with a wooden shelf and wooden cages and only one medicine: an antibiotic powder someone gave to us and which we used sparingly on the worst cases.

In the midst of the madness we tried to lead a normal family life. I bought a river boat, which we kept moored on the River Thames at Shepperton, and we had friends over and entertained. They graciously accepted the creatures deposited in cupboards and other nooks and crannies around the house. It really never crossed my mind that they wouldn't. Often we would be deep in conversation about some subject or other and Fleur would swoop in, land on my shoulder and eye up the leftovers.

Sharing the house with wildlife had other consequences that were not so pleasant. One night we went to good friends for dinner in their big, posh house in Surrey. I was sitting at the table having polished off a lovely plate of boeuf bourguignon and a couple of glasses of Bordeaux. I was listening to my mate as he recounted an anecdote about a friend of his, a trip to Bangkok and an unfortunate mix up with a lady he met in a bar. Absentmindedly, I glanced down at the sleeve of the lambswool jumper I was wearing and watched as a flea jumped off me onto the table. I glanced up to see if anyone else had noticed. They hadn't. *Should I say something or just pretend I haven't seen it?* I thought. I decided not to say anything.

In the mid-eighties the City changed a lot and it was not for the better. Something happened called the Big Bang. Markets were deregulated by the Thatcher government and trading went electronic and screen-based. The yuppie was born and a new generation of brash City boys obsessed with money and materialism like never before rode into town. In the midst of all this the job that I was expected to do became increasingly complex and the computerization of the trading environment also closed the door on one of my specialities: a process called arbitrage. The system worked like this. In different countries there were different markets – London was home to the raw sugar market and Paris was home to the white, refined sugar market. Both were usually pegged together. However, sometimes they went right out

75

of sync for whatever reason. Prices in Paris, for example, would go screaming up while London did not move. This gave you the opportunity to sell Paris and buy London at a wide differential, knowing that the real price would be somewhere in the middle and that at some point in the future, maybe a month down the line, it would come back into sync. At that point you sold your London stock, bought Paris and made a killing. I made a huge amount for the company on arbitrage. It was beautiful. I would watch for the glitches in the markets, buy what I needed and then sit back and watch the markets converge, before undoing the deal. It was quite good fun and I made a name for myself as the arbitrage king. I was one of the first people to arbitrage white sugar against raw sugar, which was ironic, really, as I was useless at maths.

After the Big Bang arbitrage stopped and, while I continued to earn good money and had six people working under me, increasingly I felt unable to understand what was going on. In part, I started to hate my working life and was relieved to get home and to busy myself with the animals.

I questioned what I was doing at work. I began to dread going to work because everything was just too complicated. The firm was also bought out by an American group and things changed. Then, in 1992, Black Wednesday happened and the City went into meltdown. The government was forced to withdraw the pound from the European Exchange Rate Mechanism and sterling dropped off a cliff. We were all at our desks for seventy-two hours when the shit hit the fan. By the end of the week the streets of London were filled with dazed yuppies wandering around like zombies, unable to comprehend what had just happened.

The job eventually took over my mind, body and soul. The firm owned me and I never had a sense of balance. My kids were half grown up, and Jill and I were living increasingly separate lives. I had done a deal with the devil and comforted myself with material trinkets and by walking around with a wallet full of £50 notes, but eventually you have to pay the piper, don't you?

CHAPTER SIX

Close the Door on Your Way Out

AFTER MORE THAN a decade I had very firm ideas about what our ethos and practices should be at Wildlife Aid. Our mission was to give our patients a second chance at a meaningful life. After rescuing and treating thousands of animals I knew categorically that the worst thing for a wild animal was for it to be kept in confinement. Wild animals live by their instincts and to cage them is to cage those instincts. In order to give the animals we rescued the best possible chance of getting back out in the wild we had to be extremely careful about the degree of contact we had with them. The worst thing we could do was to allow them to become imprinted on humans and so I put measures in place to try and avoid that happening. Human contact was to be kept to a minimum and volunteers were discouraged from anthropomorphizing, which meant not getting attached, not having favourites and not naming.

The best practice for the orphans we looked after was to wean them as fast as possible and then stop physical contact unless it was necessary for medical checks. As soon as bottle-feeding finished we broke contact apart from cleaning and feeding. No talking to the animals and no cuddling. The juveniles stayed with their own kind while they were with us and, as long as human intervention was kept to a minimum, their instincts took over when they went out in the wild.

Most controversially of all, if an animal came in and couldn't survive back in the wild, euthanasia was the kindest option. As Wildlife Aid evolved, we developed one of the strictest codes of practice of all the wildlife charities I know. While other centres heal an animal and then keep it in captivity, we do everything we can to get the patient back out in the wild and, if it would not survive, we put it to sleep. If we do have to put an animal to sleep, it is done quickly and humanely. No one takes any pleasure from it, least of all me. Often, to complete the food chain and keep the carnivorous patients familiar with their natural diet, we feed the patients that don't make it to the ones that need food. There is no waste, the natural balance is kept and, at the very least, the animals that died served a purpose to help others.

Back then, not everyone agreed with these policies. Many, I am sure, thought I was a madman. To begin with, some of the volunteers took a lot of persuading. I kept a close eye on people. I was probably reviled by some and I am sure there are still plenty in the rescuing community that do not agree with my methods. But I was resolute in my belief and over time I have been proved correct. Our success in getting animals back into the wild has been superb. Over 70 per cent of patients today go back out and get a second chance at life, which makes me immensely proud. In part, I know that is because our patients are allowed to retain their instincts while they are with us and do not come to rely on us.

As we grew, we took on more and more volunteers who had to be arranged in rotas. They learned on the job. The knowledge Jill and I had gained was passed on and I reinforced the strict rules to everyone. It was my way or no way. The volunteers are all incredibly dedicated because no one wants to clean shit out of a cage unless they are passionate about it.

The charity was run like a business and we developed systems and processes. Volunteers were trained to take down as much detail as possible about where a new patient had been found, the suspected injuries, the situation, the conditions. This was all logged and allowed us to build a picture of what might have happened. We released animals where they had been found as long as it was safe to do so. Our rule of thumb was six weeks: if an animal had not recovered in that time and was not on the mend, we knew there was little else we could do for it as it had become humanized and its instincts had begun to dull. Often we broke that rule if the animal was getting better, and, along with Fleur, some animals that had arrived in the early days remained with us, including a cantankerous jackdaw, Billy, which had been domesticated, Chippy the squirrel and

Percy the swan goose.

On the weekends and evenings, I loved the rescues and derived huge satisfaction from releases. They have always been the most rewarding thing I do. Mostly I get emotional when an animal goes back, often I am moved to tears and occasionally a release will be deeply spiritual. On one memorable occasion I was releasing a fox back into the wild. It had been brought in to us by a member of the public after being found by the side of a road, bloody and unable to walk. An X-ray showed it had broken a leg so one of our volunteer vets operated and pinned the bones back together. The animal was kept in for six weeks and healed well. I knew it was time for it to go because it had been tearing around the pen, jumping up the mesh walls. We gave it one last check over to make sure there was no infection and then I loaded it in a transport cage, put it in the back of the car and drove to woodland near where it had been found but away from the road.

I parked up and carried the cage to a clearing at the edge of the woods. Dusk had painted the sky with a kaleidoscope of reds and oranges. There was only the hint of a spring breeze and the world was silent apart from the sound of my footsteps and the fox turning in the cage. I felt totally at peace.

'You're going home, fella,' I said quietly as I put the cage down on the grass.

I wanted the release to be as stress-free as possible. I always let the animals go in their own time. Sometimes they stayed in the cage for ages before they realized they were free. I unhinged the door and propped it open, then took a couple of steps back and crouched down.

The fox scratched around for a while and poked its snout out the door, sniffing the cool evening air. Tentatively it edged out of the cage where it stood for several minutes, picking up scents and familiarizing itself with its surroundings. It took a few steps forward then turned and looked at me. As it did so, a barn owl swooped silently overhead, silhouetted against the sky. It headed into the trees and the fox, seeing the owl, took one last look at me and then followed it.

It was one of the most magical moments of my life, almost otherworldly in its beauty and symbolism. The sentimental Simon likes to think that the fox looked back in gratitude for what we had done for it, thanking us for its second chance in life and that the owl was a spiritual messenger sent to guide it. The rational Simon knows the owl was off hunting for the night and the fox was looking back to make sure I was not following.

The satisfaction I received from Wildlife Aid was in sharp juxtaposition to the increasing fear and terror I felt in my day job. I knew I was losing control when I started shaking on the way to work in the mornings. I became terrified because I felt a complete lack of understanding. I genuinely didn't know what I was supposed to be doing and what was expected of me. *I really shouldn't be here*, I thought to myself as I sat down at my desk each morning and stared at the words and numbers scrolling on the screen in front of me.

I stumbled through each day, terrified I would be found out, and by the time I got home I was in a stupor. I was crappy company for Jill and for my children, and I felt empty. The only relief I found was when I was with the animals, which provided some form of balance against the soullessness of the City. One offset the other and I was living in two very different worlds. I was 100 per cent committed to Wildlife Aid and I was happy to let it grow and grow while I oversaw it with the same commercially minded ethic that I had employed at work.

I was not sure how much Jill shared my enthusiasm for the charity's growth. In hindsight, when we moved to Randalls Farm it was probably too big for her. She never hankered after riches, recognition and status like I did. I had an ego – I still do – and without one I would not have had the drive or determination to keep moving Wildlife Aid forward. I wanted it to be the best and to do the best for the animals we took in. Jill loved the wildlife, she loved looking after the animals and she ran Wildlife Aid from the beginning, but it was all getting too big for her and I wasn't there to listen. She probably would have liked it to stay small. I invited it in and it took over our lives.

Things came to a head in 1993 when my health started to suffer from the stress I was under at work – not that I admitted it at the time. One morning I was on the train going to work and was, as usual, beset by the anxiety and terror that were my regular commuting companions. I felt hot and prickly and the next thing I remembered was coming round, slumped on my seat with a concerned member of South

West Trains' staff squatting down in front of me and asking me if there was any pain in my chest. I felt confused and worried and wondered if I'd had a heart attack or a stroke. The train staff radioed ahead and when we pulled into Sutton station there was a paramedic waiting for me on the platform with a wheelchair. By that time, I had recovered enough to protest that there was nothing wrong with me but, quite rightly, they insisted that I went to get checked out. Secretly I was pleased because I was anxious to find out what the problem was.

I was wheeled out of the station, put in an ambulance and taken to Sutton Hospital. I wasn't in any pain but felt incredibly tired and washed out. I was strapped up to a heart monitor and checked regularly. I lay there on the starchy sheets, listening to the beep of the monitor, which was printing out a record of my vital signs. Periodically, a doctor came by, looked at the printout, took my pulse and blood pressure, and went again. When it became clear that I wasn't suffering a heart attack I unhooked myself, got off the bed, called Jill and asked her to come and pick me up. She wanted me to stay in hospital and only reluctantly agreed to collect me after I told her that if she didn't I would get on a bus. Before she left home, she called our GP who was waiting for me when I got back and tore me off a strip for being such an idiot.

'We don't know what's wrong with you yet so it's a bit premature to discharge yourself, isn't it?' he said sarcastically.

Suitably admonished, I agreed to go to another hospital where I was monitored again. I was told I was suffering from 'executive burnout', which sounded very posh. Basically, I was having a nervous breakdown. I wasn't even shocked because I'd seen others suffer the same fate. Deep down I knew things had not been right: the stress and anxiety had been building for several years but I had chosen to push through it.

'Take six months off,' I was advised by a consultant, which would have been funny had it not added to my stress levels. There was no way I could go to my boss and explain that I needed a six-month break on doctor's orders so instead I took two weeks off and went back to work. There was no occupational health or assessment; I went straight back into the daily grind as if nothing had happened. I was still alive, I was still breathing and everything still worked so there was no reason to change anything. After the initial shock of the blackout wore off and I realized that I was not dying, I told myself it was a blip and carried on as normal because I didn't know what else to do. In today's working culture I would have been offered counselling, a stay in a clinic perhaps and the option of flexitime, just in case I sued. Back then, in less enlightened times, we were all appliances: if one of us stopped working they just got rid of us and brought in a replacement. People went quietly. They burned out and they were replaced, like lightbulbs.

With grim inevitability, six months later I had an identical episode and blacked out on the train again. I got checked over and after a brief break I went back to work a bundle of nerves, shaking periodically but enslaved in a lifestyle that I couldn't sustain. I had one child at private school (Lou went to Freemen's), a love of good food and a growing charity to help run.

And, just to complicate matters, I started having an affair with one of the volunteers.

The lady in question was having relationship difficulties, and Jill and I had drifted apart, but that wasn't an excuse. It was totally wrong of me. My relationship with her developed and it all came to a head because I had a PA who saw me in a compromising position with her at Waterloo station. The next day my PA took me aside and explained that, due to her ethical beliefs, she could no longer work for me in the knowledge that I was cheating on my wife. I knew that I had to tell Jill. Full of guilt and remorse, I confessed.

Jill, to her eternal credit, did not tear me apart. I had been an arse, I had betrayed her and betrayed our children. I moved out of Randalls and rented a flat nearby. We told the kids. It went as well as it could have done given the scenario. I continued my relationship with the volunteer and I also continued co-running Wildlife Aid, which obviously was based in Jill's home. News of my indiscretions spread through the volunteer community, who were rightly loyal to Jill and it's fair to say I was not particularly popular. But I didn't care because, as far as I was concerned, helping the animals was my calling so each evening and weekend I would turn up and continue directing operations. Jill and I remained separated and didn't get divorced until some years later. Life was awkward for many reasons and it got even more awkward about six months later when my tenure in the City came to an abrupt end.

One of my clients made a mistake which I tried to rectify. I was required to do the best by my client so I worked out a deal that would reverse the damage and I took a commission from it. The whole thing went sour though and I was called in and told, 'Simon, we are going to fire you', as if it was a good thing. I was given a month's notice during which time I was whisked off the trading desk and hidden in another department like a dirty secret. I hated that period and couldn't wait to get out of there. The strange thing was that when they told me I was off I felt my shoulders lift because I knew that the pressure was gone and that I wasn't going to feel scared any more.

I got a six-month pay-out, which was a reasonable sum in 1994 but wasn't reflective of twenty-three years' service. The sad thing was that after all that time I didn't get one call. I had spent more time with those people than I had done with my family but once you are out of the club you don't exist. I didn't have a plan and, as usual, had no idea what I was going to do. If necessary, I would have driven a cab. The hardest part about it all was making economies. It took me a long time to slow down my spending but the sudden surplus of spare time allowed me to devote myself fully to the animals.

CHAPTER SEVEN

The Rescuers

THE TRANSITION FROM City slicker to full-time animal rescuer was seamless. I left the City and the next day I went to work at Wildlife Aid. Towards the end of the period I like to call 'my London life' I had started to see myself as a wildlife rescuer, rather than a City worker, anyway. In London I eventually felt like a fish out of water: my natural habitat was Randalls Farm, which was no longer my home but was where my soul and spirit resided, and I was devoted to the cause that I had sweated blood and tears to develop.

The day I walked out of the City I was sure that within six months I'd have the centre financed by all my wealthy City contacts. During my notice period I had started to soften them up, dropping hints about the charity and the struggle we had raising funds. It was hard for a small charity to get noticed; we didn't have the benefit of a large back office full of support staff. I explained to anyone who would listen about the vital work we did. The numbers of patients and rescues had risen exponentially year on year; an ever increasing upward graph of misery as man trod selfishly over the natural world. Land development in the south-east had cracked on without paying much attention to the recession in the early nineties and wildlife suffered as a result. Animals were dying in their thousands on roads that continued to fill with traffic; they were choked and poisoned by litter; and driven from their habitat by diggers. The more I had seen, the more I realized that the natural world was at war with man and man was winning. I was pretty certain my impassioned polemics would melt the most ruthless commercial heart and prize open wallets. I was wrong on so many levels. Not only did none of the mean bastards donate anything, they didn't even return my calls. The day I left was the last day I spoke to any of my former colleagues, with just three exceptions. It was like the Berlin Wall going up.

Thankfully the general public were more understanding and appreciated what Wildlife Aid was doing. The local community was extremely supportive and most people got the message: that all wildlife deserves a second chance. While other wildlife charities choose to be species specific, Wildlife Aid welcomed all comers. If wildlife had been damaged by man's interference, we owed it a debt as a collective species and anyone good enough to donate was repaying some of that debt. I think the public understood and although we have never been awash with money we have managed to survive and expand as costs have increased. We had volunteers who would shake tins at local events and man stalls at fairs and in shopping centres. We made appeals in local newspapers and, with more time on my hands, I would go out with Malcolm, one of our volunteers, and help with community fundraising although I preferred corporate fundraising, contacting local employers and trying to wrestle money from their social responsibility budgets.

I was with Malcolm at a one-day event on the top of Box Hill. It was summer – peak fundraising season when all the local fairs and fetes are held. We put up a gazebo, which was lucky because it poured with rain all day and hardly anyone turned up. We made pennies; hardly enough to cover the cost of the petrol and, at the end of the day as we were packing away, a gust of wind picked up the gazebo and blew it down the steep slope of the hill.

I turned to Malcolm.

'That's the last one I am ever doing,' I told him.

To be honest, that sort of fundraising, while vital, is never going to draw in big money. You are lucky to earn a few hundred pounds here and there.

At the centre, Jill and I worked together for quite some time after we separated and I admired her for that. It was generous of her and we got on as well as we could. I dread to think what she really felt in her heart because it must have been bloody hard for her but we didn't row. For my part I carried on blithely with all the determination of a man on a mission. My motivation was twofold. Firstly, I loved going out to an animal that I knew would die for whatever reason – trapped or ill or injured – if I couldn't rescue it. I loved that I could change that animal's life and give it a second chance. It was a kick. Secondly, I loved the releases, which are amazing moments that are hard to describe. I found a balance and purpose I could not have got anywhere else and became philosophical after my departure from London. Life, I figured, was a path and the path eventually led me to where I was supposed to be. I had found my destination.

The rescuing side of the job also fed my need for adrenaline. Despite our best efforts to acquaint ourselves with the full facts, calls from the public often lacked important details and I would arrive with no idea what I was going to do or how I was going to catch something, which gave each job the element of unpredictability and excitement I craved.

'There is a deer in a field with three broken legs,' a distraught caller would say.

I'd tear over to the location (sticking to the speed limit, of course, officer) in our specially kitted out Volvo estate, which had a CB radio and one of the earliest satnavs, which had been donated by a company called Vodacom. Often when I arrived, the animal would get up and run off on all four legs. To cover this eventuality, we asked callers if they had done a broomstick test. If it was safe enough and wouldn't endanger the animal or the caller, had they been able to get close enough to the animal to very lightly nudge it with a broomstick? This helped bring to a conclusion many 'emergencies' because the animal would rouse from its torpor and run off.

On one occasion a man called to inform us he had a golden eagle chick trapped in his garden. When I arrived it was a duckling. The confusion, I assumed, was because it was yellow.

Even when I was lucky enough to have the full facts there was always no determining exactly what the outcome would be. There was no training; success depended on instinct, the ability to read the animal and the situation, and some quick thinking. My number-one priority then and now was the safety of the animal. Even if it took hours, I would wait patiently rather than risk danger or further injury to an animal. I discovered there was no skill in catching an animal. The skill was holding on to it. With deer I learned through bitter experience that you hold the antlers and keep them pointed away. Before I learned this, I received an antler in the head, which made a perfect puncture hole, and another in the neck, which luckily missed the major blood vessels.

Rescuing is about understanding an animal and adapting your behaviour accordingly. I've had volunteers who have come out with me over the years and most do not last long. Some will blunder into a situation and make it worse, others will be too hesitant and wait too long before they make a move. Today, we classify rescues according to the situation and match volunteers to the type of action necessary. If, for example a hedgehog is caught in a football net (which is a common problem), most rescuers can deal with it but if it is a 'red tag' rescue – one that is dangerous – there are only four people who can attend. You get to that level through experience and time.

Rescues have four outcomes: sometimes the animal has gone; sometimes it is a rescue release; sometimes the animal is injured and needs to go back to the hospital for treatment; and sometimes it is so badly injured the kindest thing to do is to put it to sleep (PTS, as we call it) – they are the rescues no one wanted to go on. On every rescue I am absolutely focused on the animal and the space between me and it, watching what it does and how it reacts. Sometimes it is better to take a step back and wait a moment to avoid distressing the animal. Other times I have to react quickly. It is a skill and an art and, if the creature is injured, I also need to make correct decisions about treatment. Unlike pets, our patients do not arrive with owners who can tell us the animal's medical history. We have to use detective work and experience.

Some rescues are over quickly, others take hours. Some have stayed in my memory long after they were concluded, not always for good reasons.

In the mid-nineties I was called to one of the most harrowing rescues I can remember. We received a call from the police, which was not unusual, especially if an animal needed to be put to sleep as I had a licence to carry a .38 revolver and was sometimes called to use it. It was often the quickest and cleanest way to put an animal out of its misery. On this occasion the emergency was a deer. I was told that there had been several calls over the space of a week about a deer in distress that had been injured badly in a road accident. It had survived with leg injuries and had been seen several times on the same patch of land. Nothing could have prepared me for the sight I witnessed when I drove out to the location of the reports.

It didn't take me long to find the poor creature. It was in a field bordering woodland. At first it was behind a low bush and I thought it was kneeling down on its front legs – knuckling – because its haunch was above its shoulders. As I got nearer it started to walk, which was strange for an animal on its knees. When it cleared the bush I could see piles of leaves under each front knee. For a moment I was confused until it registered. The deer had no lower front legs: both must have been severed, most probably in a road accident. It was walking around on exposed bone and each bone acted like a spiked litter picker, spearing leaves as it trod over them. God only knows how the wretched thing survived and what pain it must have suffered but it was still trying to eat grass. There was only one thing I could do in that situation. I got the gun out as fast as I could and killed it. The sight of it haunted me for days each time I closed my eyes.

Malcolm and another volunteer, John, would often come on rescues. Both were characters, as is everyone involved in animal rescue I have met over the years. The busiest times are from May to the end of August when there is a continual stream of emergency callouts and patients arriving at the centre. December and January are quiet but often the most dramatic rescues occur in these months because it is dark, the weather can be poor and usually the rescues involve an adult animal.

Over the years I became acquainted with the patterns in

nature that affect our work. Certain animals are born at certain times of the year so we get certain species in certain weeks; one week it is starlings, the next week it is foxes. I also noticed that time after time situations would be the same: for some inexplicable reason we would get a glut of jackdaws in chimneys one week followed by several deer in railings the next.

The spring is orphan season, where predominantly the patients are young animals which have either lost their parents in accidents or have been abandoned. Inevitably orphan season involves a lot of badger cubs whose parents have been killed in accidents. On several occasions I have been called out to the heart-breaking scene of a cub or cubs attempting to suckle from the carcass of their dead mother by the side of the road or by rail tracks. The youngsters are fairly easy to catch: they have a growl and a spit but as soon as they are scruffed they go limp. We take in the orphans and bottle-feed them.

We do our best for every animal and that sometimes means going to extraordinary lengths. One day, when a tiny badger cub was brought in to the centre with a dome-shaped forehead, I endeavoured to do all I could to discover what was wrong with it and get it treated. The badger was one of the first cases I'd seen of hydrocephalus, or fluid on the brain. Often sufferers are blind or have trouble walking, and inevitably they will be in pain caused by the build-up of pressure in their skulls. The condition can be congenital or as a result of illness or injury. I wanted to make sure my diagnosis was correct and I contacted Clare Rusbridge, who was a young vet and is now a leading animal neurosurgeon. She agreed to help. She called one of her contacts, a man named Henry Marsh, one of the country's most experienced brain specialists. He was fascinated by our case and agreed to see the patient. Most importantly we needed to get scans of the badger and so, with the bare-faced cheek I realized was the only way to get things done when you run a charity, I called up a posh private hospital in Surrey, which I knew had a CT scanner, and asked if I could use it. I did my homework first and found out who the right person to talk to was and then went on a charm offensive.

I managed to get the hospital to agree to let us use its scanner after hours, when there were no human patients. Then I took the badger and its scans to Henry, who looked at it and confirmed hydrocephalus. Clare and Henry then formulated a treatment plan, which involved surgery. Clare did the operation and Henry assisted because, even though he was one of the world's experts on the human brain, he wasn't a vet so could not operate on animals.

It was a Herculean effort for a little badger cub and in my mind was worth it because all life is equal. Sadly, the badger died. Interventions like that on domestic animals usually have good outcomes because owners can drain the shunt that is put in during surgery to take the excess fluid away, give the patient medication and keep the wound free of infection.

Different animal species react differently to treatment and intervention. Badgers are usually hardy but our brain patient was too poorly to survive. Roe deer have the lowest

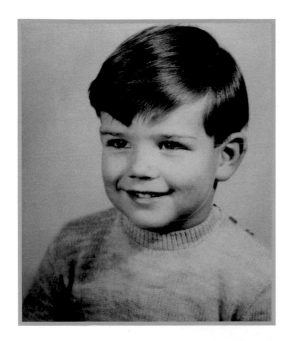

Me as a fresh-faced young boy.

Jill and me modelling a pair of Wildlife Aid sweatshirts at the door of Randalls Farm.

Me in my Wildlife Aid uniform.

Every animal matters, no matter how small.

This tawny owl was in a tight spot when we were called out to rescue it.

When I'm on a rescue, I focus completely on the animal – even when there's a camera in my face.

Percy the swan goose was one of our longest residents.

Just one of the hundreds of badgers we have saved over the years.

There is nothing more rewarding than releasing an animal back to the wild.

Below: One of the volunteers knitted a Simon for the badgers. I particularly like the attention to detail, although it should be Diet Coke.

A baby owl plays peek-a-boo with the camera.

The Wildlife Aid Foundation centre is where I feel most at home.

Sunrise on the morning after the fire showed how much we'd lost.

Various celebrities have been a great help to us. Born Free Foundation founder Virginia McKenna has been a wonderful supporter for many years.

Chris Tarrant helps out at one of our open days.

Ricky Gervais, another of our celebrity supporters, described me as 'like David Attenborough, with Tourette's'.

success rate of all. They go into a state of decline quickly. I learned early in my rescuing career that for roe deer the best option is to try and do all treatment on-site and let the animal go straight away.

Birds, too, display their own quirks depending on their subspecies. I used to say that if you worked on a kestrel it would be fine but you only had to say the word 'vet' to a sparrowhawk and it would die. Some animals are just stress-prone; woodpeckers and kingfishers are practically neurotic and have to be kept in a dark place away from people from day one. Other animals just seem to accept assistance and deal with it. I have no idea why.

The first couple of years after my untimely departure from the City were an incredible learning curve and a delight, despite the complicated personal situation I had created for myself. I was devoted to the natural world and all its wonders and would have happily rescued all the time. My financial pay-out, however, began to run low and I needed to find other streams of income. Through acquaintances I met a man called Adam who ran a video production company based in the neighbouring town of Cobham. He produced videos of school plays, polo matches, weddings and anything else that was required. I had always had an interest in photography and he was looking for someone to help him out so I worked with him to learn the trade and did some sound recording and editing. He employed a cameraman named Steve Rouse who was a larger-than-life character and we got on well. Steve was a maverick who enjoyed a drink, we shared the same sense of humour, and he was interested in the work we were doing at Wildlife Aid.

Steve knew his stuff when it came to operating a camera and some of his exploits were the stuff of legend. On one occasion he was involved in filming a conference. It was something to do with a gas or water company and involved a lot of men in suits talking about company strategy in long, dull speeches. Steve was operating a camera at the back of the room so all he had to do was make sure the shot was in focus and the microphone was pointing in the right direction. It wasn't a particularly demanding job and did not require any fancy camerawork or difficult shots. In his recollection of events, he fell asleep for a few seconds. The tape told a different story. His snoring from behind the camera could be heard getting progressively louder until the whole conference stopped and all the delegates turned around in the direction of the camera Steve was sitting behind. Someone could be heard saying, 'Can someone please wake the cameraman up?' The footage then showed someone walking towards to the camera before it wobbled when Steve was woken.

Before long I invested in my own video equipment and struck out on my own, an unplanned decision which again led me down an unexpected path.

CHAPTER EIGHT

The Good Lord Giveth . . .

WITH SO MANY well-known people in the vicinity it was inevitable that sometimes we would get celebrities coming in with animals and when they did I did my best to enquire as to whether they would like to make a donation or become a patron. If I wasn't in when they came to the centre, I would call them later.

'Hello, Penelope Keith, just to let you know, the animal you brought in to us is doing well. Have you ever thought about making a donation? I loved you in *The Good Life*, by the way.'

Charities, I soon learned, needed all the help they could get.

In the mid-nineties I happened to meet Chris Tarrant. It was just before he became the host of *Who Wants to be a Millionaire?*, the hugely successful quiz show. He and his then wife Ingrid were both animal lovers, and Ingrid was particularly interested in animal welfare. They lived nearby and we talked about my work and how the charity had started and they were both fascinated. Chris, who had led a bit of a wild life himself, enjoyed some of the more outlandish stories I recounted and he had a great sense of humour. I turned on the charm and persuaded him to become a patron. Over the years they both gave their time and support unselfishly and Ingrid still helps out today.

I like Chris a lot. He is a nice chap with a wicked sense of humour and he offered to do what he could to help us out. He was a valuable addition to our growing band of celebrity patrons, the first of which was Sir Harry Secombe, whom I persuaded to come on board when we first formed the charity. I had been at school with Harry's son and knew him vaguely although we hadn't spoken for some time. Still, that provided enough of an introduction and Harry was happy to lend his name to our efforts, as was Chris, who agreed to appear in a Wildlife Aid video appeal. Increasingly, I was getting interested in the opportunities video footage provided us and I devised a plan to make an advertisement-cum-appeal. We could send it out to people and use it in our promotional material. We could put it online, too, but in those days internet speeds over dial-up meant that people would have to wait an age for it to download.

I wanted the film to highlight the most common type of incident we got called out to deal with: we attended scenes of road accidents involving wildlife almost daily. Each year we were taking in scores of badger cubs, orphaned when their mothers had been struck by cars.

Chris came into the centre and narrated the appeal with a badger on his lap. We edited in scenes of a mock-up accident and finished the video with some scenes of injured deer and rescued fox cubs as Chris explained that, with the increasing number of roads and road users, wildlife was under threat and Wildlife Aid needed help. Now. Please.

For an early attempt at my own production I was quite pleased with the results. It was powerful. I could just as easily have filmed an ad full of baby animals in various states of cuteness, which arguably would have received a better reaction. As unpleasant as the truth is, however, wild animals die every day as a result of our actions. We stomp over the planet with no regard for it or the creatures on it, and there is no point trying to deny that our actions have unpalatable consequences.

The more I used the camera equipment, the more I saw the potential. I picked up techniques quickly as I'd always been a fast learner. I started touting for production myself and began a business in video production, filming plays for local primary schools so parents could keep the videos for prosperity. It was easy work because the set-up involved only one camera. As long as the angle, view and sound were right, there was little that could go wrong.

I started taking a camera with me on rescues, too, and sometimes Steve would come along and film with me.

Several volunteers had asked me to teach them rescuing techniques and it was not the sort of job that you could teach from a textbook or easily explain. They wanted to know the ingredients for a successful rescue. Mostly they wanted to come out with me in order to learn, but this was logistically impossible, especially if it was a 2 a.m. rescue. I always tried to keep my response time to about four minutes – a target I keep to this day – from the time the call comes in to the time I leave. I wrote down the details, assessed what kit was needed, collected the kit together and went. I couldn't hang around waiting for volunteers to arrive so I could give them on-the-job training. Filming the rescues meant that I would have a stock of footage to show potential rescuers at a later date when I could sit with them and explain why I did what I did in a given situation. The footage not only allowed people to see techniques for catching different species, it also allowed volunteers and budding rescuers an insight into animal behaviour in the field.

The footage was popular because, in the majority of scenarios I filmed, there was drama, emotion, tragedy and, often, comedy. There were rescues on water where I'd be flapping around in a pond in the small plastic boat we had, or rooftop rescues where I'd be terrified. Some were full of dark humour.

On one occasion I was called to rescue a squirrel stranded on a roof. It was on a house by a main road and I drove there with my camera in tow.

'It's been lying on the roof for three hours,' the owner had explained when she called through. 'I don't think it is dead but I can't be one hundred per cent certain.'

Sure enough, when I arrived with a volunteer, the squirrel was lying face down on an apex roof. It was motionless and

I assumed the homeowner's suspicions were correct and the poor thing was indeed dead. I couldn't be sure, though, and as I never walked away from a rescue knowingly without a conclusion, I knew I would have to go up and investigate properly.

'I tell you what I'll do,' I explained. 'I'll go back to the centre, get the ladders, come back, climb up and have a closer look, just to make sure. If it moves in the meantime call me.'

The round trip to collect the ladders took another hour, so by the time we returned the squirrel had been motionless on the roof for well over four hours. It also started to rain and the poor thing was soaked. It had surely carked it, otherwise it would have got itself out of the rain.

'I'm afraid this is going to be a recovery operation,' I told my colleague confidently as I climbed the ladder.

The squirrel was lying near the lip of the roof, just above the gutter and remained unresponsive to the sound of the ladder clanging against the eaves as I climbed. I concentrated on my grip and footing as I climbed up the back of the house, by which time a small crowd had gathered in the road to watch the daring man pluck a dead squirrel from a roofing tile. Eventually I cleared the guttering and came face to face with the animal. I was so close to it and our faces were level. Its eyes were closed and its little legs and arms were spread-eagled. It was completely still and couldn't have looked more dead. I lifted my hand carefully and slowly reached over to confirm its demise and as I did its eyes opened with a start. We both jumped, and I let out a curse. In one burst of energy, it shot off across the roof, leapt into a tree, ran down the trunk, across the garden, over the fence and into the road, straight into the path of a bus which braked hard to avoid him. He was last seen heading off into a thicket somewhere near Epsom.

Videos of similar exploits built up into a video library that people loved watching and one day an acquaintance, Brian Cardy, made a suggestion. A friend of his knew a man called Michael Atwell who was working on the new terrestrial television station, Channel Five, which was due to be launched the following year, 1997. Michael commissioned arts- and feature-based series for the channel and was high up in the company structure. Just getting a meeting with him was a coup.

Brian's friend put in a call, explained what Wildlife Aid was doing and told Michael about our videos. Michael agreed to meet. I edited the best of the footage into two tapes; each was roughly an episode long and had some narration over the top – they were rough edits (known as rushes in the production industry).

Michael invited me to his office in central London and, as we sat down over a cup of tea, I explained about Wildlife Aid and our work. We then sat in his office with the blinds pulled and watched the videos I'd brought. Halfway through I looked over – it was at the point of a particularly emotional rescue – and I saw Michael's eyes glistening with tears.

He's crying, I thought to myself, *which can only be a good thing*.

When the videos were finished Michael took a deep breath.

'I love it,' he gushed. 'Can we have a series?'

'No problem,' I answered, without thinking.

To add some context, TV production companies work tirelessly developing programme ideas and the whole process can sometimes take years. They shoot and reshoot, they employ staff and high-end production techniques, they edit carefully and they build relationships with commissioners (the people at television channels who decide whether to buy a programme or series). Negotiations can go on and on. To get a series commissioned by a terrestrial channel is a big deal. In contrast, I had a short meeting and showed some roughly edited tapes and was offered a deal there and then. Once again, fate, luck or circumstance – call it what you will – had intervened. I hadn't even been out of the City for two years and I was wet behind the ears when it came to television production, but I had achieved something much more experienced television producers rarely get to do. I had been awarded my own series.

After the congratulations and the hand shaking were over, Michael asked me a question.

'How are you going to do it?'

It wasn't a question I'd given much thought to. He wanted to know how we intended to produce the episodes. We were not a TV production company. We were a wildlife charity. We had the cameras but no high-end editing equipment and we didn't have the ability to turn the raw footage into a finished television programme with tight editing, soundtrack and titles – the part of the process called post-production. Normally, an independent production company would film the subject and make the show. That would have been completely impractical for me. Ultimately, I was a wildlife rescuer not a television presenter and I didn't harbour any ambitions to become one. I certainly was not going to let a television crew get in the way of my work and I was aware that if I used an independent company they would most likely have a different set of priorities to mine. It was fine when Steve filmed with me because he understood that during rescues the welfare of the animal was the most important focus and that always had to remain the number-one priority. When he filmed he stayed out the way and allowed me to get on with my work. If I could talk to the camera or give the camera a better shot without distressing the animal or jeopardizing the rescue, I would, but he never asked. A production crew with a sensationalist agenda would.

I wasn't going to miss the opportunity, however, so I lied. 'I have my own production company,' I explained. Michael nodded. I'm not sure if he smelled the bullshit or not.

We went through the details. The working title was *Wildlife SOS*, a name that stuck for sixteen years. Briefly, we worked out a time frame. It was spring 1996 and the channel went live early the following year so the series would need to be ready by then. We were given a budget. Channel Five was not awash with money. It had only allocated £110 million a year for programming, significantly less than the ITV network's £600 million and Channel 4's £270 million at the time. *Wildlife SOS* was the cheapest show the channel commissioned. Our first series budget worked out at around £5,000 a programme. With that I had to pay staff, pay for post-production, buy equipment and cover costs. It didn't leave much, but it left enough for me to live on and to keep the charity going.

When I got back to Randalls Farm that afternoon I walked jubilantly into the office and shouted: 'I need a production company now.'

Then I called Steve.

'Get your arse over here. We have a TV series to make.'

Over the following days I set up my own production company, Wild Productions. I went out and bought the kit we needed and I made a deal with a company nearby to post-produce the series. Steve came and worked for me and we started filming.

Steve and I got on well, and he understood my ethos and the way I worked. We had a laugh when we could but the situations could turn on a pin and he knew when it was time to be serious. To begin with Steve was stationed at the centre five days a week. He lived nearby and when there was a particularly dramatic night rescue I called him and he could be at my doorstep in minutes.

I was given advice from an executive producer named Paddy Haycocks who was a senior executive of factual programming at Talkback Thames. He had been working in the television industry for over thirty years and had extensive knowledge of news, features and documentaries. He'd worked at every major broadcaster and so offered us guidance and experience.

People were a bit surprised when I arrived with a cameraman in tow. Today, we always ask if people mind being filmed but in the early days we just turned up and shot the rescue and it seemed to work. No one complained and many people enjoyed the opportunity of being in a television show.

We took the tapes to be edited in batches but I was never happy with the post-production. In fairness to the company that did it, my City habits had died hard and I had beaten them into such a good deal in my favour that it wasn't in their commercial interest to spend much time and effort on the shows. They just wanted to knock them out quickly – churn and burn – whereas I knew we had better footage and the early shows could have been improved if more production time had been spent on them.

I never had any training to be a presenter. I was probably useless at the beginning. I had been fine explaining things to camera when I thought the footage would only be seen by volunteers but those early pieces to camera for the series were excruciating. I felt that I was being stared at. The camera came up and I had a tendency to back away, like a threatened animal. Paddy gave me a bit of media training but it went straight in one ear and out the other. I improved with time and dropped my posh City accent.

To me the transition from rescuer to rescuer with a TV show seemed effortless. It was fun and I enjoyed doing it. I could see the big picture and realized that the TV show would give Wildlife Aid the sort of exposure and platform of which most small charities could only dream. I didn't stop to consider that anyone else might not feel as positive about the new direction as I did.

In hindsight, I was perhaps inconsiderate. To suddenly make the Wildlife Aid centre the focus of what was essentially a fly-on-the-wall documentary was a big ask for those who were also involved there, not least my broken family. The situation between Jill and me was still delicate. We were separated. The farm was her home. Gemma and Lou were living there too. The volunteers were mainly on Jill's side and most probably thought I was a monster. I had split up the family but still loomed large over the empire Jill and I created. And I had decided to turn the gaze of a TV camera on it all.

CHAPTER NINE

. . . And He Taketh Away

WE HAD BEEN filming for six months and everything was going well. There was no end of drama to capture on video and I was confident that the material we were getting would make an engaging television show. Some volunteers refused to be on film while some lapped up the opportunity. Jill was gracious and was involved in the show: as co-founder of Wildlife Aid it was important that she played a role. Lou appeared, too, while Gemma chose not to.

We started filming in the spring of 1996 and had been flat out all spring and summer, our busiest periods. We had shot hundreds of hours of tape, capturing everything from the sublime to the ridiculous. As I had hoped, Steve and I continued to work well as a team because he knew how to get what he needed for the series without getting in my way and I helped the camera angles when I could. On some occasions, when I needed an extra pair of hands,

Steve would put the camera down and help out, which was what I expected of him. The wildlife always came first and we tried to be as honest as we could with what we filmed. Sometimes we would film the set-up shots (showing me driving or walking to a location and discussing what was happening) and panoramic location shots out of sequence or after the animal was rescued or released because it was more practical. Often, once the action was underway I could not stop what I was doing just to narrate.

On one occasion we filmed a badger release in a place called Westhumble near Box Hill. We released the badger at twilight and he was slightly sedated so it took him longer than I expected to leave. By the time he had wandered off back into the wild it was too dark to film the set-up shots we needed.

'It's fine, we'll come back tomorrow,' I said.

The following night Steve, a couple of volunteers and I got in the car and drove back out to the site where the badger had been freed. For continuity we needed the exact light levels from the night before, which we had recorded. When we got there and checked it was far too light and we needed to wait until it got darker.

'No point sitting out here,' I said. 'We may as well find somewhere to wait.'

The nearest place was a local country hostelry so we went there with all our equipment and an empty animal transport box and ordered drinks. Then we ordered a few more. For some strange reason it took a long time to get dark that evening and by the time it was dark enough I was slightly tipsy, which made the walk back to the site in the fading light over banks and rough terrain interesting. I was stumbling around in the gloom while everyone else laughed. It took a while for everyone to compose themselves and just as I was about to start my narration someone farted and we all started giggling like children again. I managed to keep it together long enough and then announced to the camera that it was time to let the badger go. The plan was to film me leaning down and reaching into the cage, at which point we would edit into the shots from the previous night of the badger wandering into the woods.

I held the box by the handle with one hand and reached in with the other. As I did I shook the box a bit to give the impression that the badger was scuffling around inside.

'He's lively,' I said to the camera as I reached in.

The light on the camera went out as it stopped filming.

'Is it a take?' I asked Steve.

'No, it's not, you knob,' he replied.

'Why?' I asked.

'Because the badger was sedated. You were shaking the cage as if it was active!'

On another occasion I was called to a water treatment plant after a worker there had spotted a bird in one of the tanks. The message came through from reception: 'Bird stuck in waste tank.' I went with another cameraman I knew at the time and, as we drove to the rescue, I had my fingers crossed that the tank in question was fish-tank sized and that the waste was water run-off. As we neared the plant the smell that greeted us dissolved my optimism.

'It's a bloody sewage plant, isn't it?' I said grimly.

The vast waterworks consisted of several huge concrete vats sunk into the ground, each around 12 metres across. Within each one water purification was taking place. Raw sewage came in and was pumped through the system, becoming cleaner and cleaner until it was clean enough to be put back into the river system.

We were met at the office by a member of staff who explained the problem.

'It's some sort of black bird and it can't get itself free and it's in the middle of a tank. It really is in the shit,' he explained wryly before leading us through the plant. The smell was cloying – it hung in the air and made my eyes water. The guy with us seemed impervious to the stench but I was constantly fighting the urge to vomit. I supposed years spent in that environment had burned away his sense of smell. I don't think I've smelled anything as bad since. Even the most infected wound would have been favourable.

He led us to the side of one of the tanks, which contained a dark cocktail of effluent, not quite solid, not quite liquid. In the middle sat a coot, flapping forlornly and spraying crap over itself with its wings.

The cameraman and I looked at each other.

Normally, such a rescue would require the long net I carried in the car. However, at full extension it was only about 2.5 metres and wouldn't be long enough to get near the poo-covered coot.

'We'll need something longer,' I said. It was evident that the rescue needed to be done quickly. The fumes were making me feel queasy so heaven knew what effect they were having on the bird. We raced back to the car and shot off to the nearest town where we found a hardware store and bought a bundle of bamboo poles. Back at the sewage plant we taped them all together using a rescuer's best friend – gaffer tape. We taped the lengths of bamboo to the net and managed to extend the reach by another 2 metres or so.

I fixed myself to the railings that ran around the side of the tank with a harness to stop myself falling in and leaned over the edge with the net and poles raised above. Then I dropped them in the sludge as near to the coot as possible. The contraption was unstable and so long it bent easily. The bird was too weak to move away but I couldn't get the net in position. I pulled the net back, dragging through the sludge, carefully shook it out, taking care not to splash myself, and repeated the same action, trying once more to get the net near enough to the bird to allow me to catch the thing. It took several attempts, but each time the net and poles splatted into the tank with a plop. Eventually I managed to get the coot in the net and pulled it back across to where I was standing. I think it must have known that we were there to help it because it didn't struggle. It was covered in slurry. I pulled it out of the net and grabbed hold of it but it was slippery. Before I could get a good grip it gave its wings a vigorous flap, which covered me in a shower of excrement.

The cameraman did his best not to laugh and I did my best not to swear. I quickly wrapped the coot in an old towel and put it in a carry-cage before it could do any more damage. The guy who had shown us to the tank had been watching the rescue and thanked us as we took the bird away. I detached my net from the poles and handed them to him.

'Can you get rid of those for us please?'

The coot was taken back to the centre where it was checked over, cleaned up, fed and given the chance to rest in our rehab pool. It was released somewhere safer and cleaner a few days later.

By then the centre had developed enough to allow us to take in hundreds of patients. The biggest rehabilitation area was the 'top barn' at the end of the garden.

Inside we had dug a badger sett into the ground. The barn was also used for storage, including food for the patients which was kept in freezers. Parts of the barn had also been divided into various pens and aviaries. It was linked up to the office with CCTV so anyone in the main house and office could keep an eye on what was happening there.

Although I wasn't technically living in the farm, I spent a lot of time there. It was my castle. I had built it and it was where I felt safe and calm. No matter how chaotic things got outside, inside or in my personal life, I always felt in control when I was there. I didn't like being away from it for long periods of time. I often stayed in the office into the night, catching up with the more mundane things you have to do when you run a charity. Sometimes I was with Steve or some of the volunteers, sometimes on my own. Jill and the girls were usually there and there were always people coming in and out because the centre was a twenty-four-hour operation.

I was there, working late one evening in the autumn of 1996 when I heard urgent shouting outside. I ran out to see what the commotion was about, looked up and saw the sky at the top end of the centre glowing red. I could smell the smoke, which was billowing into the sky. Fire! I went on autopilot and ran indoors to call the fire brigade. They arrived within six minutes and in that time I ran up see what was happening and, when I saw the top barn ablaze, I started ringing as many people as I could to get them in to help. We had about thirty volunteers at the time and I tried to call all who lived nearby. I called the vet we used, too, as I feared she would be needed.

'There's a fire, come now, we need help.'

Lou later recalled that she rang Steve. She was in bed because she wasn't feeling well and remembers waking up and seeing the blue lights of the emergency services as they arrived. She looked out her window and saw two or three engines already there. She couldn't work out whether the fire was in the house, the coach house where my parents lived or in the centre. Then she looked up and saw a huge red-orange glow and realized the top of the garden was on fire. By the time she was dressed and out to help volunteers had arrived.

After rousing as much help as I could I ran to the top end of the garden to start the rescue operation. Jill was there, too.

Firemen were running around, laying hoses and telling everyone to get back. They used the pond as a water supply but, despite the rapid action, within only minutes the fire became an inferno. The barn and the structures around it were wooden and although it had been a damp evening, which may have slowed the blaze, the fire was fierce and getting hotter.

Along with the volunteers I started to walk into the fire zone.

'You can't go in, it's too dangerous,' a fireman shouted. All I could think about were the animals that were trapped there as the fire started to creep towards their pens. There was no way I was going to stand back and let them perish without trying to help so I ignored the advice. There were around sixty animals of all descriptions in the pens and I was determined to save them. I ran through an open door and all around was smoke, fire and heat. Others followed me. I went into pens, grabbed animals, put them under my arm and ran out. There were around five of us, darting in and out of the enclosures, dodging flames, and the fire crew did their best to damp us down. Each time one of us emerged we were sprayed with water and the firemen tried to create safe pathways into the building so we could get to the stranded patients.

Fleur was in one of the aviaries attached to the barn and there was a padlock on her door. The fire was spreading so quickly that I couldn't go looking for the key so I grabbed the nearest heavy object I could, which was a paving slab. I lifted it above my head and smashed it down onto the lock, which snapped off. I kicked the door in, ran in and grabbed her. She was cowering on a perch, and the flames licking at the walls were reflected in her huge, terrified eyes.

Up and down the path we ran, gathering the patients we could and placing each saved animal in any available pen away from the danger zone. There were ferrets, birds, foxes, hedgehogs and deer carried to safety. None of the animals put up a fight when we went in to get them and, because time was of the essence, to begin with we put animals in any pen just to get them somewhere safe. We put animals together that would have eaten each other in the wild. Foxes went in with pigeons, owls went in with hedgehogs, but not one predated or attacked another. They knew the situation was serious and knew to behave.

In all we saved scores of patients in a remarkable rescue operation that took hours while the firemen continued their work. After around an hour they had the fire under control and we started moving animals on the periphery out to other pens to get them away from the smoke and fumes. It took all night to reorganize the centre and, after the patients were out of danger, the volunteers began the process of checking their health. In the end, of all the creatures that were there, we lost just three.

Throughout the night I had been worried about the sole badger in the sett in the barn. I prayed that because he was underground he had managed to survive and, once the blaze was out, I went inside the remains of the barn and started digging to get to him. Others helped and, after their shift was over, some of the firefighters also returned. It was hard going because the heat-baked earth was rock hard. It took several hours and was getting light when we finally got to the ante chamber the badger had dug for itself in which to seek sanctuary away from the heat and smoke. It was around 2 metres down and the ground around the sett was still smoking and hot. Carefully I bent down and reached into the hole we'd opened up around the patient and I saw him move. I was hit by a wave of emotion.

'It's okay, fella, we're here to get you out,' I said.

I was choking back tears and couldn't believe that after such a ferocious fire he was still alive. I slowly pulled him out, taking care not to hold him too tightly in case he had sustained burns. I carried him to the hospital where, under better light, it became apparent that he wasn't in a good way. Although he had no visible injuries, his breathing was laboured, most likely as a result of smoke inhalation. He was put on oxygen and I left him in the capable hands of the vet. I returned to the ruins. Steve was still filming and as the sun came up he captured the most moving shots of the smouldering timber and fractured, dripping water pipes.

Everyone had been running on pure adrenaline and as it started to wear off tiredness set in. I stood in the ruins on my own for a moment and felt a sense of crushing loss. I felt like a general surveying his defeated army after a bloody battle. It was silent except for the dawn chorus and the hiss and crack or water dripping over charred timbers. I had built the centre, it was my life and here it was smouldering in ashes. Tears stung my eyes as I looked around and thought, *This is insane, I can't rebuild all this again now after all the effort and work.*

I felt exhausted but knew there was so much more to do, so I went back to the office and started calling as many media organizations as I could. I wanted people to know what had happened. I called the actress and wildlife campaigner Virginia McKenna and she agreed to come down, there and then, to help out. Within hours news crews were parked outside and were filming the remains. I did interview after interview and Virginia spoke on breakfast TV about the tragedy.

At some point that morning we looked back over the previous night's CCTV to see if we could pinpoint where the fire had started and what caused it. We found the seat of the blaze easily. It began behind one of the freezers. The footage showed it going from a little bit of a flame to a huge blaze in a matter of minutes. I didn't realize at the time but as a deep freeze gets older it runs hotter. The top barn was a dusty environment and a bit of straw, hair or fluff had probably got caught in the back of the machine and burned. I've since learned to pull out fridges and freezers every six months and vacuum round the back of them to make sure they are clean. Some lessons are hard learned.

Through the day other volunteers started to arrive and we organized a clean-up operation. At one stage I tried to lift up the paving stone I had used the previous night to smash open Fleur's door. I couldn't even get it off the ground. It is amazing what adrenaline can do.

The whole custom-made area at the top of the centre had been gutted and the more I realized how much we'd lost, the more I thought about giving up. It was a rough few days and the worst time came when the vet walked into my office a few days later to explain that the badger we'd saved had succumbed to its injuries and died. It was my moment of wobble. I felt at that point lower than I ever had. I was bereft for a while and just needed to take myself away to try and process what had happened, make sense of it and come to terms with it. All the while patients were still coming in. Some had even arrived the morning after the inferno. They didn't stop just because we had a disaster. The volunteers were heroic and made sure that, despite it all, there was no disruption to the service we provided.

My moment of doubt lasted several days while the smell of charred timber still hung over the remains. And then the local newspapers came out with the story on the front pages and my faith and optimism began to return. One by one we started getting envelopes in the post. Some had cheques, some had cash. People called to offer help. We had cards from well-wishers. We hadn't even started to actively fundraise to replace the buildings and yet people sent money.

One lovely old dear, who lived up the road and must have been in her eighties, saw the story on the news. She walked all the way up the road in the cold and gave us a £50 note. That single gesture of kindness absolutely choked me up. It still does when I think of it. That lady could have spent her money on anything but she thought what we did at Wildlife Aid was important enough to merit it.

Several days after, the insurance assessors came and were extremely helpful. It became apparent that, with the insurance payout and the public's generosity, we would be able to rebuild. The interest in our story lasted a week or so, and then it was old news. When all the fuss had died down, we collected ourselves together, dusted ourselves off and started working out how to move forward. As usual, I didn't have a plan in mind. I trusted that things would come good.

Christmas passed and we welcomed 1997. It had been a decade since we had become a registered charity and I was optimistic about the future. We carried on shooting *Wildlife SOS*. I still have the camera from the first series, which I will never sell. It's the box Brownie of video recorders, a plastic MS1 SVHS camera, like VHS but better quality. In the early part of the year the publicity drive for Channel Five's March launch swung into action. It was the first new terrestrial channel for fifteen years and *Wildlife SOS* was one of its first ever programmes to be broadcast. Our little wildlife show was introduced by the Spice Girls. Immediately the series seemed to strike a chord with the public. I like to think that it was my charisma and good looks that carried the show but in reality they came second to the animals and the stories of dramatic rescues.

My moment of doubt was long gone and, as the months went on we started to rebuild what we had lost. The top area of the centre was rebuilt virtually identically because it had worked. We added more CCTV cameras, which meant we could monitor animals without approaching them or going in their pens. This distance was vital for their recovery and reintroduction back in the wild. We also rebuilt the badger sett but made one important difference. We created an above-ground sett which, while not ideal and not faithful to badger habitat in the wild, did mean that if in future we needed to get to the animals quickly we wouldn't have to dig them out.

The work continued for several months and while I usually used volunteers to get a job done I wanted the rebuild done properly and I didn't want it dragging on so I employed professional builders. Demand was increasing all the time and I wanted Wildlife Aid to be able to cope. To everyone's credit we replaced everything that had been destroyed within a year.

CHAPTER TEN

Onwards and Upwards

BEING ON TELEVISION meant I had what is laughingly referred to in the media world as 'a profile'. Consequently, I became a go-to expert whenever other television shows were doing features about wildlife and Bill Odie was unavailable or Chris Packham wasn't answering his phone. Being on other shows allowed me to raise awareness of Wildlife Aid and our work so I was happy to oblige. Even before *Wildlife SOS* I had been filmed for news items on several occasions – including once when a ferret I was holding memorably shat down my arm. That footage still does the rounds on *It'll Be Alright on the Night*.

I appeared on daytime TV with Fern Britton on a couple of occasions and each time was asked to take an animal – a hedgehog once and then a badger. If I was asked today I wouldn't comply because it is not fair on the animal. You live and learn, and back then I thought it would be good publicity. The hedgehog was taken in to illustrate a story about hedgehog numbers in decline in the wild and I was on the sofa with Fern holding it without gloves. In the middle of the live programme the hedgehog decided to bite me on the finger. I carried on talking to Fern and the camera didn't pan down to show the carnage that ensued out of shot. I could feel blood trickling down my hand and I was being asked questions but all I could think was, *This really hurts*. Mercifully we went to an ad break and I managed to prize the creature off my hand and clean myself up.

On another occasion we were on air talking about badger cubs. Fern wanted to give a hug to the badger I had taken along. The cub was an orphan and was being bottle-fed at the centre. It had just been fed so it was settled but, like all babies after milk, badger cubs puke. As Fern cuddled up to the baby it let out a small badger burp and puked on her left breast. I was holding a towel that the badger had been wrapped in and without thinking I leaned forward to wipe the milk off, reaching out towards Fern's rather ample boob. Out of shot, as I leaned over, two security guards leaped out from the side of the set. I stopped before I made contact. They obviously thought I was going to grope her live on TV.

On another occasion I was asked to do something on Sky News with *Songs of Praise* presenter Pam Rhodes. I took Fleur and had the owl on my shoulder. In the middle of the interview, she decided to hop onto my head. I am follicularly challenged with little cover up top so I could feel Fleur's talons on my scalp, which was bearable. Suddenly, however, a light burst in the studio and Fleur tensed up, which meant her grip tightened and her sharp claws punctured my head. I could feel the blood dripping down my neck and grimaced through the rest of the interview.

Even on the occasions when film crews came to our centre things did not always run smoothly. We were filming in the garden once with a fox and, while I held it, it bit me on the thumb. I tried to release its jaw with my other hand and it bit that instead. As I walked away to clean myself up I still had the radio mic on and the crew overheard me cursing and threatening to go back and wreak revenge on the little monster (which obviously I never would have done). I dropped myself in trouble with a BBC news crew, too, when I forgot to take off my mic during a hedgehog news item. The producer with that particular crew was asking for some ridiculous shots.

'Can you put it down there and get it to walk over this way towards the camera?' he requested.

I stood there rolling my eyes because it was a wild animal and you cannot tell wild animals what to do. The producer kept trying the same shot again and again and eventually, after I pointed out that I was no longer going to risk stressing the animal, they agreed to go with what they had. I was exasperated by then and as I walked away to put the hedgehog back in its pen I muttered to myself what a complete bunch of unmentionables I thought they all were.

'Sorry, we don't mean to be,' said a voice in my ear. I had left the mic on and the soundman had heard my tirade.

Being on television also meant I was recognized by my first fan, an eighty-year-old lady with no teeth in a supermarket. She was a fair representation of my fan base. My dreams that lots of pretty young groupies would fling themselves at me never turned into reality. I did get fan mail, however, and over the years have had correspondence from all over the world. I received an email from the United States just recently from a kid who said he loved *SOS* and wanted to be a vet. He set up a Just Giving page to raise funds for Wildlife Aid, which I thought was wonderful. I have always endeavoured to make time for people who are interested in what I do and can't understand people who get famous because of the public and then choose to ignore them or, worse, deride them.

The show also boosted attendance at the annual Wildlife Aid Open Day, which we had begun to hold each summer. During the day we opened the centre and invited people in to allow them to see what we did and to meet some of the patients. The event got increasingly popular and also became an important part of the fundraising calendar. One day, I bent down at 11 a.m. to sign an autograph for a child and didn't get back up for three hours because the queue was so long. We started the open days in 1995 and they became my guilty pleasure; my one day of fame.

Meanwhile *SOS* continued to gain popularity and was commissioned for a second series but I became increasingly dissatisfied with the post-production. Using an outside company also meant I was having to go backwards and forwards to a studio to do voiceovers. My relationship with the company became fractious and, around the same time, my friendship with Steve soured so while he continued to work on *SOS* things were awkward. I took production of the series to another company, Cloud Nine, in Dorking, and also tried to find more staff because Channel Five had doubled the amount of shows they wanted from twelve to twenty-four. And to complicate matters further I was no longer seeing the girlfriend with whom I'd had the extramarital affair but was living with another woman, Paula. She had supplied us with radios for an event we hosted and I struck up a relationship with her. She was the antithesis of Jill, all of which made me rather unpopular at Wildlife Aid once more.

Into this maelstrom of crap stepped a young man named Jim Incledon, a film student who wanted a job as a cameraman and whom I found by chance. I had asked the new production company whether they could recommend any junior camera operators and someone there knew a lecturer on the film course at Plymouth College, where Jim was studying. The lecturer put Jim in touch with the company and I agreed to give him a go. Jim explained later that before he came to Wildlife Aid for the first time he went to Cloud Nine for the lowdown. As he explains it, he was told there was a crazy man in charge of a TV series going on some sort of self-destruct personal rampage at a wildlife hospital in Surrey. He was told my life was in freefall because I'd left home after having an affair with a volunteer; my ex-wife was still living at the centre where I worked; I had another girlfriend; my daughters weren't speaking to me; Jill wasn't speaking to me; and Steve Rouse, the main cameraman, wasn't speaking to me.

With hindsight I can see that there is truth in this assessment of the situation, yet I was in my own little world. I guess I knew to a degree that the situation was shaky but I had faith that things would come right in the end.

After his meeting Jim drove over to Wildlife Aid and I wasn't there. He met Steve, who looked like Hulk Hogan and hated me by then. Everyone Jim met hated me and told him what a monster I was.

He was shown to a desk and, while he waited for me, he decided to call a friend and explained excitedly that he'd landed a job on a TV series and was going to get his name on the credits. After five minutes Jill went storming into the office and started telling him off because he had been using the house phone and not the office phone. That was his first encounter with her. I eventually turned up later in the afternoon and laid down the law like a sergeant major, telling him what I expected and that he needed to be able to keep up. He called me sir, which made me laugh. I imagine by that point his head was spinning and he was wondering what on earth he had let himself in for.

Before I went I left a camera on his desk and explained to him that I sometimes filmed my own rescues on it. One of his jobs was to log any footage I had acquired that could be used in an episode. Jim took it and, when I left, put the tape on to start watching. Unfortunately, I'd forgotten that the tape in the camera was not rescue footage. On the previous weekend, I had been staying at the Waterside Hotel in Bray with Paula and the footage consisted of tastefully framed shots of her in the bath. Poor Jim thought it was some sort of weird test and spent half an hour rewinding and forwarding the tape to make sure it was in exactly the same position it had been when I had given it to him. He didn't tell me he'd seen it for several months.

Jim turned out to be a brilliant operator, a real friend, one of the family and also a good laugh. Everyone loved him. Lou and Gemma got on well with him and he became like a brother to them. As the work was 24/7 and he had nowhere to live he lived in the house for several years before deciding he wanted his independence; he bought a camper van, which he parked in the driveway at the front of the house, and lived in that before he finally rented his own place in Leatherhead.

We went out on our first rescue along with Steve, who was still at the centre for a while after Jim started. Jim, eager as a newbie, had everything carefully organized. He had a big new cameraman's jacket on with stuff in each pocket. He had spares for everything. The location was a country house called Juniper Hall and we had been called out because there was a fox in trouble in the grounds. Night was drawing in as we pulled up to the house. I told Jim to get out, run ahead and take a shot of us driving up the sweeping gravel driveway. He leaped out the door and sprinted ahead, and as he did everything in his pockets fell out. The next morning Jim had to go back and pick up bits of kit he'd not had time to look for the previous evening.

We had two slogans: 'We can polish a turd' and 'We can drink anyone else under the table'. Jim was very exacting and professional; he would get frustrated with me when I muttered my personal slogan, 'We will just wing it', which I said all the time.

We worked well together but had moments when we got cross with each other. He would accuse me of shooting everything in soft focus. Theoretically, I was his boss as I was series producer but he called the shots and by the end of the series we had become good mates and knew how each other worked. With extra staff I was able to take on other private work. We did school plays and corporate gigs, and placed an ad in wedding magazines enticing customers to have their weddings filmed by a top television broadcast crew. The weddings and corporate work made more money than the TV series. A wedding could net anything up to £3,000 and a school play could bring in £2,000. I had black polo shirts printed up with the Wild Productions logo on them for us to wear and, depending on the job and number of crew required, I hired in outside help. As I had a mixing desk I could also do live events such as conferences, where we would have several cameras linked in to the desk and a director controlling things. We did a big event for Office Angels and a friend, Steve Knight, manned the mixing desk while Jim, Lou and I worked the cameras. The action took place on a stage around which a set had been built. At one point I started to climb up a staircase to get a good overhead shot and suddenly heard Steve shouting in my earpiece.

'That's not a real staircase, it's part of the set. It's not stable.'

I could hear Jim and Lou laughing in their mics as I carefully edged back down.

Later during the day someone wandered in front of the back projector that had been set up for the event and I heard Lou exclaim loudly: 'For fuck's sake, move your arse.'

The guilty party answered: 'Sorry!' It was Jonathan Ross.

We filmed one huge wedding in the first ever marquee designed without a centre pole. It was on a farm and the field in which it was erected had been mowed so closely it looked like a lawn. Inside the marquee the father of the bride, who was a very wealthy businessman, had recreated a Covent Garden Market scene. All the food they ate that night was on the stalls: the fish, the fruit, the meat. We filmed for seventeen hours and it was a spectacular wedding but hard work because the cameras were not light. As the slow dances started at the end of the night I was exhausted. I was filming on a handheld camera on my knees, shooting upwards from a low angle. As I went to get up after the song, I realized that I couldn't move either of my legs. I panicked and thought I'd had a stroke. I called for Jim who came running over, looked at the pitiful sight in front of him and started laughing. I'd forgotten that I was wearing shoes with Velcro straps, which had stuck to the carpet. The night was topped with a huge firework display and one of the spent rockets fell on the marquee roof and started a fire. Luckily it was put out before it caused too much damage.

CHAPTER ELEVEN

Gunslinger

EVENTUALLY THE *WILDLIFE SOS* series made a seamless move from Channel Five to the Discovery Channel and Animal Planet, and was shown across the world. There was no shortage of animal stories. There are plenty of people out there who, although good natured, are slightly nuts and will happily call me out on a wild goose chase. Often the old and confused make a beeline for us and some situations repeated themselves year after year. For example, every January calls come in about wild animals in distress, howling and screeching in gardens and parks. The volunteers or I have to explain to the caller that the noises were foxes and they were far from distressed because January and February is fox-mating season. They were, in fact, having a lovely time and the last thing they needed was a wildlife rescuer arriving on the scene and spoiling the fun.

One of my favourite ever calls came from a woman who phoned in with a fox emergency.

'Some horrible person has glued two foxes together and they are in an awful lot of pain,' she explained.

I asked her the details and she told me that they were joined backend to backend and had been running around together for around an hour. Whenever one went to run away, the other was dragged along with it howling in pain.

'How could people be so horrible to animals?' she exclaimed.

I was smiling on the other end of the line, not because I took any pleasure in the thought of an animal in discomfort but because I knew what had happened.

'You don't have to worry,' I told her calmly. 'It is mating season and it sounds to me that they have been a little too vigorous in their activity. The male is stuck.'

I could sense her face reddening as I explained tactfully that foxes and dogs are prone to a situation called 'dog locking', which happens during mating when the male's swollen penis gets stuck inside the female. I can only imagine how painful that must be for the male and how inconvenient for the female but the best thing to do in the situation is to let nature take its course.

We are not always able to solve problems over the telephone, however, and sometimes questionable call-outs get through the system. Jim and I attended one such 'emergency' soon after he started when an elderly lady called in because a bird was trapped in her loft. Loft rescues always provided good footage because I hated heights and I hated climbing up ladders. There was also the real prospect that at some point, if I was bounding around in someone's loft, I might fall through the ceiling, which would have added to our tally on *It'll Be Alright on the Night*.

When we arrived at the house the lady explained that she could hear the bird chirping loudly and that it had done so all the previous night, keeping her awake. As she showed us up the stairs and onto the landing I could indeed hear a loud noise, but it wasn't a bird.

'Madam, are you sure your smoke-alarm battery doesn't need changing?' I asked.

'Oh,' she said, 'is that what it is?'

The alarm was beeping a low-battery warning and after she'd apologized profusely for wasting our time I went out to the car, got a nine-volt battery and changed it for her, at which point the noise stopped.

Some people have mental-health difficulties and I find that, with them, it is often best to go along with whatever delusion they are suffering. Often they are just lonely, troubled people who want a bit of contact, like the guy who rang up and said he lived next to a school and there were snakes in his garden. Now, snakes are the one thing that I do have a bit of a phobia about and, although I have handled several and would not hesitate to rescue one, I derive little pleasure from them. I was apprehensive on the drive to the call but felt compelled to have a look just in case. When we arrived the gentleman was standing in his garden looking around frantically. He was only young, probably in his thirties.

'What seems to be the problem, sir?' I asked as I walked up his garden path.

'Look at all these snakes,' he said.

There were no snakes but he was completely serious.

'There's a bird with a coat-hanger in its mouth, can't you see it?' he added.

I could see he was clearly troubled and instead of walking away I pretended to look around and helped him pick the imaginary snakes up off the lawn. He really believed they were there and I didn't think it would help him to argue they were not.

Another time, a man came in looking very upset and carrying a shoebox.

'It's a worm,' he explained to the receptionist. 'I cut it in half by accident when I was mowing the lawn.'

She didn't know what to do or say so she called me. I came out and inspected the worm, which was indeed in two halves.

'We'll be able to save at least one of them, sir,' I explained. 'We'll bury the other one respectfully in the earth – it's what he would have wanted.'

In fact, with such a large volume of work, inevitably some animals don't make it. As I mentioned, where it is appropriate – if there is no disease and drugs have not been used – we keep some of the dead as food for other patients. We can't bury the rest because there are too many, and there are also health and safety rules to abide by. To deal with the issue I made an arrangement with a nearby animal cemetery and crematorium, which kindly offered to incinerate them for nothing. Subsequently, one regular job for a volunteer is to deliver the sad cargo of dead animals to this establishment. Sometimes, if there were no volunteers available, the job fell to Jim or a cameraman I employed later, Phil Broadhurst.

We also set up two big incinerators at the top of the garden to dispose of the muck from the pens. Each day there were barrows full of poo and bedding. The ash from the incinerator was used on the fields as compost and any clinical waste from the hospital was taken away by a specialist disposal company. As we expanded it became a struggle to comply with all the rules and regulations but, because we were on television, we had to be doubly careful to do everything right. Applying for our public liability insurance alone was like writing a book. As our volunteers were dealing with wild animals the policy had to have special clauses in case they got scratched by something or bitten by something else.

Over the years I witnessed so many hard-to-stomach situations that, like every paramedic, police officer and doctor I knew, I started to develop a gallows humour as a defence mechanism. I saw death every day and tragically over the years had to put to sleep many, many animals. On countless occasions we did everything to try and save an animal, spent time and resources giving our all to heal it and it died. If you let all that sadness build up with nowhere to go it would finish you off. That is why anyone who does a similar job where life and death is often in the balance always has a dark sense of humour.

Even the horror of being called out to shoot an animal that has been mortally injured in a road accident sometimes provides moments of surreal laughter. One night, I was in the office with Jim when someone from Surrey Police called to inform me that on a road there was an injured deer that was still alive but had sustained several broken legs and was in pain. It was likely that I would have to shoot the animal. A handgun is better than a bolt gun and more practical than a rifle. I would put it to the head between the eyes and fire. As soon as the first shot rang out, the animal would be dead. The cameramen were always shocked when they saw me shoot for the first time – it was never a pleasant thing to witness and I always felt grotty afterwards but I would know that I had done the right thing.

On the night in question Jim and I had both had a few glasses of wine so I explained to the police officer that, while I was happy to help and capable of performing the task, I wasn't in a fit state to drive. They sent a car for me and Jim and I sat in the back, with my pistol in its case. When we got to the scene I got out the car and was getting the gun ready. The deer was on the ground in front of me and the copper in charge was standing in front of the deer. As I pushed the rounds in I explained to the police officer who was in the line of fire that he might not want to stand where he was. I slurred my words ever so slightly for comic effect and Jim started giggling, which then set me off too. The policeman very quickly moved out of the way and got behind me.

I once took one of Lou's boyfriends along with me on another shoot request. His name was Angus – a musician with dreadlocks. I wasn't overly keen on him and when we arrived at the stricken animal I asked him to steady its head by holding its antler while I did what needed to be done. He was white as a sheet afterwards and didn't say much on the way back. It was a Godfather-type warning.

SOS continued and I employed an American editor called Jason to make a team of four. Jim, Phil and Jason were all in their early twenties and were all dedicated and professional. We made a good team and also tried to have fun when we could because the workload was incredibly demanding. Sometimes the boys, as I affectionately called them, would try and add a bit of inappropriate humour to the edits we sent off to the channel and in their downtime would edit together some of the unusable footage. In one episode we were filming a peculiar condition that some hedgehogs suffer called subcutaneous oedema, or balloon syndrome. If a hedgehog sustains a certain type of injury the cavity under their skin can fill with air and they inflate. It can be caused by respiratory damage or by gases produced by a deep wound. The hedgehog can inflate to the size of a football and, like a puffer fish, go completely spherical, which looks slightly ridiculous when they roll around and flap their legs. The only way to deflate them is to insert a catheter and squeeze out the air. We filmed an example for the show and Jason found it so funny that he put a comic sound effect of a deflating balloon over the top and a tiny, soft voice in the background saying 'pleeeease kill me'. It was almost imperceptible and he forgot to take it off when he sent it to the channel, who missed it and broadcast it.

With the television show, the volume of work and the general madness I rarely had the chance to step back and reflect on the impact Wildlife Aid was having. I loved seeing the wonder on children's faces during the open days and I started to do public speaking and school visits in an effort to spread the word and raise awareness of the importance of wildlife. My mental age is probably around seven so I was happy talking to seven year olds! I loved talking to kids in schools because I knew I could walk away from them and I didn't have to look after them for the next fifteen years. And children get inspired by wildlife. I started to realize that if I could get to kids between the ages of seven and fourteen and make them interested in nature and wildlife then perhaps I could make a difference. I saw how important education was. By the time we get older most of us are brainwashed to go out to work and make money with no regard for what our lifestyle is doing to the planet we inhabit.

It isn't only children who gain a sense of wonder from wildlife. One day a representative from a charity for the blind based in Surrey called and asked if it would be possible for some service users to come to the centre. One of their staff was a fan of the show and thought it would be beneficial for the people. I couldn't see the point initially and was probably quite blunt with them but agreed anyway and we decided to film the visit. A small group arrived, all visually impaired and some completely blind. One chap had a stick with a bell on it. They were all excited and we lined up a selection of animals for them the encounter and feel. I was a little worried that something might nip a finger or they might get pricked by a hedgehog spine but they were all incredibly dextrous and seemed to sense the animal in their hands. It was wonderful to watch and any cynicism melted away.

One man pulled me aside and said, 'I have never seen an owl', which was an interesting use of language. So I went and got Fleur from her aviary and held her up for the man to touch, guiding his hand towards her. He started gently stroking her and I put her on his arm so he could feel how light she was. The look of wonder on his face was unforgettable. It was a new experience for him and thankfully he couldn't see my reaction because I was choked with emotion. When the boys edited the footage they faded the scene to black just with sound, which made it even more poignant.

CHAPTER TWELVE

Goodbye, Dad

AS EVERYTHING CHANGED there was always one reliable constant. In the background there was Dad who quietly went about the place, helping people and animals and fixing the stuff that needed fixing without ever needing to be asked. Dad's DNA was in the centre just as much as mine and Jill's, and he guided us from a distance. He always had time for everyone. He was the most gracious and selfless man I knew and I probably didn't tell him enough how appreciated he was. He was there to help us rebuild after the fire and felt the loss as keenly as any of us but never made a fuss about it. He watched proudly as we set about making our television show. He helped the volunteers and built new pens and enclosures as we expanded. On sunny days he liked nothing more than to sit by the pond and watch the geese and ducks. He had a special bond with Percy, who was his favourite creature.

In many ways Dad was my shadow. We were close and he had been the guiding influence in my life, teaching me to think around problems and to be self-sufficient. I loved him, he loved me and we never needed to talk about it. He had always been the most amazing support. In the late nineties, nearly twenty years after we started the centre, Dad was still there, slowing slightly in his old age but as helpful as ever. And then he got ill. It started with a persistent cough that got worse. He got tired easily and he started to look frail. I knew early on when we went to the Marsden that he had lung cancer. It took six months, which in a way was a blessing because he didn't suffer for years, but it was still too long and the last weeks were awful. My dad died in 1998. He was seventy-eight and I still miss him.

You may have worked out by now that I am not prone to mawkishness when it comes to human relationships. I can cry my eyes out when I release an animal and often do but with people it gets complicated. Dad and I didn't discuss our emotions but as he neared the end of his life I wrote him a letter because I wanted him to know what I felt and what I thought of him and how grateful I was for what he did for me. The letter wasn't discussed but at least Dad died knowing how loved he was.

At the end of his illness we brought him home and he spent his last months at Randalls Farm, the place he loved and the place he built. It was a very fast deterioration and the last week was horrendous. The only saving grace was that the cancer had spread to his brain and he wasn't aware of what was going on. For those of us who loved him it was hard to watch. My dad had been about 67 kilograms, all bone and muscle, very fit and wiry – he could lift things that I couldn't – but he became a ghost shuffling around, exhausted and burdened with an illness that weighed him down. It chokes me when I think of it.

He was in bed at home at the end. It was tough. When he finally slipped away there was a Macmillan nurse with us. She came up to me to put her arms around me but I threw her off. It wasn't the nicest thing to do but I needed to deal with it myself, in my own way. If ever I am troubled or sad I go off somewhere, deal with it alone and tell everyone later. After Dad died I got on with things, I tried to punch through to the other side but every day something would happen that reminded me of him and I would get blindsided by emotion. I kept thinking about it, about him, about his last months and about how the farm and the centre were never quite the same after he had gone. I hunkered down and dealt with it because that's the preservation instinct I have. My mother also suffered and I didn't ask for support.

I used to be terrified of dying when I was young. I would get myself in a state if I let myself think too much about death and what comes after because I couldn't handle the grim reality of mortality. Over the years my attitude changed; if you are going to die, you are going to die; it is going to happen at some time or other and there is nothing you can do about it. I was never religious when I was growing up, even though I was in the choir. However, later in life I started to formulate ideas. I am sort of religious now but it's my own version of religion. My church is going out and doing a rescue at night, which is when I am at peace. I believe something created everything. It may not have started with Adam and Eve, but something started this off, some universal force out there that makes it all happen. In the early nineties I started to look for things to make me less scared of death and I discovered reiki. I did a course and in the end I became a reiki master. I will use it on people if I am asked to. I don't talk about it much but I believe as a healer you are a funnel with the ability to channel energy into someone and give them the belief and ability to heal. The human brain and body are an amazing, self-healing bit of kit.

By the time Dad was cremated I'd sorted things out in my mind. I had said my goodbyes and I didn't want to do it again so when his ashes came home to be scattered on the pond I took a step back. Mum took him up to the pond to do what she had to do. She tipped his ashes into the water and they spread across the surface. As they did Percy jumped in, thinking that it was feeding time, and started to peck at the remains.

'Stop eating Michael,' Mum was calling.

As I said, I am not prone to mawkishness but in a way it was fitting. Things that died were sometimes used to nourish things that lived; it was the natural cycle of life and Dad really loved those birds anyway.

My relationships with people were always more complicated than my relationships with animals. I had lots of personal friends but many were colleagues and I never had quite the same relationship I have had with animals, particularly my dogs. Don't get me wrong: I'd do anything for my friends and family and am loyal to the end. If one of our staff or volunteers rang me up at two in the morning and said something awful had happened, I would be there in a flash.

But if you asked me about the most significant relationships in my life, aside from family and girlfriends, I would say that my rescue dog Sam was my soulmate. I've loved all my dogs over the years but Sam was a kindred spirit. After I got him it took me a year to calm him down because he was psychologically damaged from the situation he'd been in. I had been looking for a dog and, through a rescue and rehoming service, I heard about a couple who were getting divorced and were looking for a home for their golden retriever. I arranged to see him. He'd obviously witnessed rows and was very nervous because when I went into the garden I lifted my arm as if to scratch my head – I did it on purpose to test his reaction and gauge his temperament – and he hit the deck. It was a sure sign that he was scared of humans. I knew he needed to get out of the environment he was in, and I was calm and measured with him. We connected. Animals are very instinctive and Sam could sense that I was not going to do him any harm – he came with me and got in the car without a problem.

I was renting a house in Leatherhead with Paula at the time and Sam had adjustment issues when I took him to his new home. He tried to kill other dogs quite regularly for the first year and he bit Paula on the arm, which turned out to be the turning point for him. He went for her when we were together, teeth gnashing, showing the whites of his eyes. We were in the lounge and quick as a flash I grabbed two cushions from the sofa and went towards him, using them as a barrier. He backed off and I hit him with them, not hard but firm enough to get him into a corner where I kept him until he calmed down. He wasn't happy and was snarling at me but it was a defining moment because he realized I was the alpha. From then on he was much better for the rest of his life. With troubled dogs sometimes there is a defining moment where their brain kicks into place and they realize where they are in the pecking order.

I slowly trained him and he was always on a lead when we were out and there were other dogs around. Gradually he came to realize that he was safe and the aggression – which was a defence mechanism – was replaced by a slight lunacy, which was endearing. You can't change the damage that has been done to an abused dog overnight. Sometimes it can take years and it is not the dog's fault. If there is a problem with a dog, you can bet it's people that have done something to it. Sam worked through his issues with humans and became a real character. We had a fireworks display at the farm for Lou's twenty-first birthday and he got it into his head that he was going to try and bite a roman candle that had been lit. The crazy dog grabbed it out of the ground and started running around the garden with it in his mouth. I was screaming blue murder at him.

'Sam, put the fucking firework down!'

The guests were jumping out the way and Sam was trying

to eat the firework as it was exploding. How he didn't injure himself I will never know.

My relationship with my dogs has always been very different to the relationship I have with wild animals. I respect them, too, but for different reasons and in different ways. All animals have characters, even small ones. A while ago we had blue tits nesting in a box and we rigged cameras up to it to watch them. One day I sat in my office and I watched this pair of birds going backwards and forwards with food for their young. Their determination was heroic. They must have gone backwards and forwards a thousand times because the chicks inside were about to fledge. Their work-rate and devotion were absolutely phenomenal. They were only small birds but they showed a huge amount of character. And then one afternoon I saw that the chicks were gone, which was strange so I reviewed the tape to see what happened and it showed that a woodpecker had drilled into the box, pulled them all out and killed them all. That was hard-core – nature at its harshest – but I can guarantee those adults would have nested again somewhere else and started the whole process over. The whole centre mourned the loss of those fledglings because they had captured everyone's imagination. The raw cruelty of nature often caught us unaware. I have done several rescues with members of the team that have not turned out well for the animal and on the way back we haven't talked at all because we are so emotionally drained. The job is a roller-coaster of massive highs and lows and, while I hate the lows, the highs make the sad outcomes worth it.

I came to terms with the death of my dad and life went on. Mum stayed in the coach house and Jill, Lou and Gemma helped look after her. Aside from Dad the biggest death that affected me was my cousin, David, who was only in his early fifties when he died. He had been like a brother to me and I had spent many happy days with him on the farm in Essex when I was young. When his wife called one day out of the blue to tell me he had passed away suddenly I was shaken to the core.

A year after Dad died life changed again. I had been living in rented houses with a succession of girlfriends while I continued to work at Randalls Farm every day, driving Wildlife Aid forward, expanding it and making it bigger. Jill and I worked together. Then, in 1999, Jill decided she wanted to move back to Gloucestershire to be near her parents. Perhaps my dad's death had made her re-evaluate her relationship with her own family. Before she moved out we decided to finalize things and got divorced. She treated me well in the settlement considering it had been my fault and I will always feel guilty to a degree for the way I treated her. She remarried several years later and was very happy, which eased some of my guilt.

When Jill moved out, I moved back into the farmhouse, which I had always seen as my spiritual home. It made perfect sense because the girls, who were in their mid-teens, were still living there. It was a seamless homecoming. I had very little to bring back. Jill moved out one day and the next I came in with a couple of suitcase and a bit of furniture. The disruption for the girls was minimal. They both helped out around the centre and were beginning to develop their mother's love of the arts. Jill and I never pushed them into anything and left them to make up their minds about what they wanted to do but, funnily enough, they both ended up doing things I would have liked to have done. Gemma went on to be a brilliant actress. From school she went to college and studied drama. She toured with theatre productions and had roles in various plays. Sadly, it's an industry in which talent only gets you so far and luck has a big part to play. She trained as a fitness instructor as well, and developed a successful business as a personal trainer. Lou developed a career as a singer and songwriter and got a deal with a record label.

SOS continued to raise awareness of the work we were doing. In some ways it helped to boost fundraising but the daily effort to keep the centre afloat financially continued to be a struggle. In the charity sector there is a hierarchy of causes; animals are in the bottom 5 per cent and within that wildlife is lower than pet charities and domestic wildlife is at the bottom. People love wildlife but I found that did not translate to donations. They took the wildlife around them for granted and would rather give to causes related to sexier animals such as elephants or tigers. I got letters critical of the show, accusing me of spending the charity's funds on television production. I replied to each one to explain that it was the broadcaster that paid for the costs incurred.

A low point came when we were investigated by the Charity Commission, which had received a false accusation of financial irregularities at the charity. The investigation cost Wildlife Aid £12,000 in accountants and lawyers' fees just to prove the claims were unsubstantiated. Then we were investigated a second time, again after further claims, and again we were exonerated. It was a nightmare. They sent in a forensic accountant but thankfully I had always made sure our accounts were carefully kept and in good order.

When I left London I thought running a charity would be cushy compared to the corporate world. There is a great deal of bitching between charities as they try to compete for a diminishing pool of money. Several years ago I talked to other wildlife groups about creating a cooperative of charities to boost our influence and resources. The system would have allowed us all to save costs by sharing the expense of vital functions like fundraising and public relations. The plan fell on deaf ears, however, because everybody was so scared that there would be a bloodbath when a £5,000 donation came in, with the charities fighting to get a chunk of the money. There is some honour among wildlife charities, however. We share information and help each other out with patients and advice. And we are all more networked today because of social media.

I guess we are lucky to be based in an affluent part of the country. Sometimes people offer money when we save something from their garden but what saddens me is that, usually, the wealthier the people, the less they are likely to give. Someone came in a beaten up Austin Maxi, brought in a pigeon and gave us a fiver. A few days later someone else turned up in a Ferrari Testarossa with an injured hedgehog and gave nothing. However, I couldn't be too critical because at least he cared enough to bring it in.

We try our best to make people aware that when they bring in an animal it costs money to look after it. There are posters up in reception and our receptionists are very good at giving the message without being too obvious. If I am in reception, I sometimes try and use humour.

'Unless you become a Wildlife Aid member I am going to kill this animal,' I have been known to say. Or: 'Unless you donate a fiver we will not give this animal its medication.' My staff apologize for me. I do it jokingly but hopefully the member of the public understands that underneath there is a serious reason. Sometimes, though, they walk out with a confused and shocked look on their faces!

CHAPTER THIRTEEN

International Rescue

I WAS NEVER AN avid television viewer, even when I was on the television. If I did ever sit down and watch something, it would usually be a chick flick. There was something about rom coms that helped me relax and switch off. However, in 2001, a television show started that caught my attention, mainly because of its chief protagonist and co-creator.

Pop Idol came out on ITV and as a family we were interested because at the time Lou was taking her first steps towards a career in music. As a singer-songwriter the show went against all her beliefs, offering singers the chance of instant stardom without putting in the hard graft or learning the trade. My interest was mainly in the head judge, Simon Cowell, a fellow animal lover, who became the most famous man in the UK thanks to his brutally honest style of critique. He was a divisive figure. Like me, he was a version of

Marmite; you either loved him or you hated him because he said exactly what he thought and he didn't beat around the bush. He was the nation's pantomime baddie. If you were obese and you couldn't sing he'd tell you and often he didn't bother with diplomacy. I liked the guy. And of course we shared a name, which in some roundabout way did not do me any harm. It was easier to get tables at restaurants and I could legitimately call myself 'Simon Cowell, the man from the television programme'. Being older than him I could also lay claim to the name as I had it first, although over the years, as his profile went stratospheric, I inevitably became known as 'the other Simon Cowell'. Apparently, he lived off Diet Coke and Marlboro Lights, like me, but I just wish I had his bank balance.

While I personally didn't have the other Simon Cowell's financial clout, Wildlife Aid did manage the monumental task of raising enough finances and resources to replace the ageing hospital unit, which was based in the front part of the house, with a new, purpose-built, state-of-the-art veterinary hospital outside in the grounds. It was opened in 2002 and was one of the best equipped hospitals for wildlife in the country. We had full digital X-ray facilities that were better than those of most vets. We had ultrasound and pathology equipment that allowed us to do blood tests. We had everything that commercial vets had and in some cases more. Much of the equipment was donated. Our X-ray machine cost £12,000 and was donated by Animal Friends, the insurance company. We also had two oxygenators, which were paid for by Exxon Mobil.

Some people would baulk at the idea of taking money from a company that operates in the oil sector, but in my opinion it is a question of degrees. If I was offered a million pounds by a vivisection company I wouldn't take it, even if that offer was made without the requirement for publicity or endorsement. My red line is animal abuse. However, when it comes to other sectors you have to be pragmatic and look at offers on a case by case basis. If companies have money in ring-fenced charity funds, that money is going somewhere, so why not to us?

The whole subject of donations is a minefield. Should an animal welfare charity take donations from a pharmaceutical company that tests on animals? Some would say definitely not but where do those principles take you? Do you use their drugs on the animals you are trying to save? Do you refuse to buy their drugs even if they are the cheapest and most effective? Should companies test cosmetics on animals? Of course they shouldn't. Should they test medicines on animals? If my child was dying and the one drug that was going to save her had been tested on animals, of course I'm going to want her to take it. It is a judgement call at the end of the day and, whatever your decisions, you will inevitably upset someone but you can't let your own high principles become a straitjacket to your higher purpose. Running a charity is a long game and you have to give yourself all the advantages you can. To survive, charities have to engage with the corporate world and that inevitably creates grey areas.

The new hospital meant we needed to increase our veterinary cover. We used a pool of volunteer vets to staff the hospital and called in specialists when we needed certain surgical procedures. We also needed a permanent vet nurse qualified to carry out minor procedures, give injections and administrate and coordinate all the vet functions. Having a vet nurse would also help me on rescues. They could carry out first aid *in situ*, lessening the need to bring an animal back to the centre. The result would be more rescue releases, which was our ultimate goal.

Our first vet nurse was Sara Cowan. When she came in for an interview I explained to her that we were also filming a TV series and that, if she agreed, she would feature in it. She was slightly nervous about the prospect but agreed. She was very good at her job and was good company. She worked for us for seven years and came on countless rescues with me. We worked closely together and inevitably shared a lot of emotional scenes because of the nature of the work. It is far more difficult being a vet nurse with Wildlife Aid than anywhere else because they not only have to deal with a lot of patients, they also have to deal with animals that they have not seen before. There are no owners to explain medical histories. The vet nurses also have to deal with 320 volunteers who are all slightly nuts!

It is sometimes lonely work running the charity and treading the fine line between trying to keep things afloat, trying to keep the volunteers happy and staying true to my beliefs. Often, there is little thanks and much fire-fighting. In 2005, however, I was recognized for my work and was awarded an MBE for services to wildlife, which was an honour. One of the newspapers reported that the award was for 'servicing wildlife'. I rang them up and demanded a correction, in case anyone thought I was a pervert.

I felt the award was as much for the volunteers who have made Wildlife Aid what it is as it was for me and so, rather than go to Buckingham Palace to receive it, I arranged for it to be awarded in a ceremony at the centre where everyone could be part of the occasion. I was delighted to be made an MBE and still hanker for the opportunity to get a platform where I can champion the environment. A lordship would be superb but perhaps I'd be better suited to a damehood – so I could throw gladioli at everyone!

By 2006 the production team felt that the series needed to step up a notch. The rescues were often dramatic but the animals and situations started to become familiar – after eighteen pigeons in a row we needed something fresh! We started to talk about making a foreign special. In truth, the motivation was nothing more than an effort to spice up the show and allow me the luxury of fulfilling a lifetime ambition of going on safari. I had always wanted to see animals such as lions and elephants in the wild and had never travelled very extensively. I'd been on holidays over the years but never anywhere particularly exotic.

Initially, Jim was sceptical. There were a lot of logistics involved in getting a camera crew and all our equipment abroad and we needed to cost things carefully. There was also no guarantee that we would get the right footage as we only had a set amount of time in which to film. In the UK, we could easily take our gear out and film everything every day; abroad, we had at best a week to get enough footage to make at least one episode. It took more arranging and that inevitably fell to Jim who, without the benefit of any local knowledge, had to do watertight research to make sure the whole thing worked.

I used my powers of persuasion.

'Come on, Jim, we can have a holiday while we are there and if things go wrong we'll wing it.'

Jim researched the best location, Zambia, and the best operator, Norman Carr Safaris. The company's history and ethos fitted well with that of Wildlife Aid. Norman Carr established the first safari camp in the Luangwa Valley in 1950, back in the days when an African safari was a hunting experience. He developed the pioneering idea of taking people to look at animals and photograph them, rather than to shoot them. His first safari camp was set up in partnership with the local tribespeople and he involved them in the management of the wildlife, an idea that was way ahead of its time, encouraging the traditional owners of the natural resource to take responsibility for its usage. His pioneering approach proved to be the forerunner to a cornerstone of modern-day conservation policy.

We arranged to stay at Kapani Lodge, which was the company's headquarters and Norman's last home. It was located on the banks of one of the Luangwa River's many ox-bow lagoons close to the main Mfuwe area of the South Luangwa, one of the finest national parks in Zambia. We planned out a shooting schedule and set out not only to show animals in the wild but also to highlight some of the perils they faced in the form of poaching and trapping. We had five days to film and while we were there also took a trip into South Africa where we filmed at another wildlife rescue centre.

We didn't use local fixers like other television crews because we were producing the show ourselves. People in the animal conservation and rescue world tended to respect us because of what we did in the UK. I made sure that everyone who ever worked on *Wildlife SOS* shared my beliefs and the principle that the animal always comes first. All the team – Jim, Phil and Jason – would drop the equipment and help out if they were needed and didn't think twice about getting involved in the hands-on stuff if needed. In the worldwide community of wildlife rescuers we were fellow nutcases. We were kindred spirits. We all loved what we did, we were all passionate and we all had that dark sense of humour.

We managed to juggle budgets and flew out for our first experience of international rescue, staying at a game lodge by the water's edge in an idyllic part of Africa, close to nature. We were incredibly lucky when we got there because we were the only visitors. It was off-season and the company gave us our own driver and guides. We had a great time and saw some amazing stuff. Due to the limited timeframe we made sure we packed in as much as we could. Every day was like three days because we went out on safari in the morning, in the afternoon and again at night.

There was all manner of wildlife wandering around. On one occasion Jim went off to his bungalow in the dark after dinner and a few drinks. He had a torch to light his way. He came back white as a sheet a few minutes later. He'd encountered a hippo on the way, which was just standing there, blocking the path and looking at him. Hippos are attracted to light and can also be very aggressive so Jim switched off the torch and legged it back to the bar where he had a few more drinks and waited for the interloper to go on its way.

Personally, I found the whole experience was cathartic. I had watched plenty of documentaries about African wildlife on television but had no idea just how beautiful and moving it would be in real life. The screen doesn't truly encapsulate what it is actually like: the sights, the colours, the sounds and the smells. I spent a lot of time in awe of it all. One day we sat by a watering hole, which had shrunk as it was the end of the dry season. There was a giraffe over on one side, a lion lying in cover on another side and a croc basking in the middle. All the animals had eaten and drunk and appeared to be enjoying the sun. It all fitted together. Everything had its space. It was amazing to watch nature in balance. Obviously, when the sun went down they all tried to kill each other but for that special moment they were all there in harmony.

The filming went well. We interviewed gamekeepers, conservationists and the local people who knew the animals best. We filmed a family of elephants in the Luangwa National Park. Every day they made a journey across a river to the other side of the park to forage and then, as the sun started to set, they went back to their original location. Many years ago, before the whole area became protected, the abundant food was in an unprotected part of the park.

My first foreign filming
assignment to Zambia
was an amazing
experience.

In Vietnam with our government minder and the crew: Jim, me and Jason.

To be so close to one of the world's rarest creatures was an honour.

I talk to Dr Marker about her scheme encouraging goat herders to protect flocks with dogs, rather than guns.

In Namibia at the Cheetah Conservation Fund with Dr Laurie Marker.

Wildlife SOS gave me the opportunity to see other conservation projects around the world.

Amazingly these seals made their own way to the seal rescue centre when they were ill.

Rescued penguins in South Africa prepare to go back to the wild.

Filming in Russia where the wild wolf population is in decline.

In Belize where this baby croc had found its way into a hotel. Luckily the staff there called in the experts.

British Veterinary Ophthalmology specialist Dr Claudia Hartley investigates a Vietnamese moon bear for eye disease.

Nothing can prepare you for the sight of a great white shark emerging from the murk of the ocean.

Rescued elephants in Thailand.

The elephants learned that poachers operated there at night so they would eat there in the day but go back to the safer area as it got dark. The behaviour was conditioned from hundreds of years ago.

On one occasion a bull elephant from the herd took an interest in our open jeep and wandered up to get a closer look. It was huge and cast a long shadow over us as it walked towards us. Although it didn't charge, it certainly had the intention of checking us out. I couldn't tell if it was aggressive or not so I took my cue from the reaction of the rifle-carrying guides who were with us. The fear on their faces indicated there was something wrong. In such situations I worked on the premise that the experts knew what they were doing and when they got twitchy, I got twitchy. Then one of the men started to go through his pockets to get bullets out to fire a warning shot, which did little to reassure me, especially when the chap dropped them on the floor. Scarily, the elephant got close enough to touch before it realized we were no threat and wandered off.

On another occasion we were in a vehicle in the middle of the savannah when an elephant saw us and suddenly started to flap its ears in an aggressive manner. It was a long way away but it was obvious that he'd noticed us. We did the same as we would do on any rescue where the animal was aggressive, and slowly reversed away.

The footage we got from Zambia and the excursion to South Africa was superb and added a new dimension to the format of the series. What most people didn't realize was that there should have been a crew of about twenty people doing what our small team of three or four managed to do. We did everything between us, we did it well, we all cared about it and we all mucked in.

In a way, Zambia changed my life. Seeing animals as they should be seen – in the wild at a distance – reinforced my views on a range of wildlife issues. Just having the time to appreciate nature is so important. We don't allow ourselves that luxury nowadays and inevitably we lose sight of the value of the natural world. It's rare for people to sit in the garden for half an hour and experience the wildlife around them. Everyone is too busy to appreciate the world so we don't notice it when it is in trouble. We'll wake from this stupor one day and realize it has all gone.

CHAPTER FOURTEEN

Lion King

I NEVER MAKE MUCH fuss about my own birthdays and special occasions because I am always on call and focused on the work at the centre. The truth is that I never really relax but I never feel the need to because I am at my happiest when I am working. Even Christmas Days have been interrupted over the years as I was called out to rescues. We have volunteers in but when they go home the phone diverts to my mobile. It is the same on birthdays. I have usually worked. Which is why one year, when we received an unusual call on my birthday, I went off to investigate without a second thought.

Jim took the call and came in to the office with the details.

'There's a woman in Cobham who says she bought some exotic fruit from a greengrocer and when she got it home a huge spider crawled out of it and is now hiding under her furniture. She says it looked like some kind of tarantula. It should be a good one for the TV. I'll get the equipment.'

Phil was with us and we loaded up the car and sped off to a small unit of maisonettes above some shops. Initially, I knocked at the wrong door and shocked the old man who answered. When the mistake had been rectified we eventually reached the correct address and the door was answered by a very attractive woman, who appeared quite flustered and explained to me what had happened.

'This thing jumped out of the bag of kumquats and ran under the sofa. I was screaming. It was as big as a hand,' she said.

'Don't worry, madam,' I reassured her. 'We'll find it.'

She ushered us inside to the lounge and pointed to where she thought the spider was hiding. While Jim and Phil were filming I got on my hands and knees with a torch and started looking around under the sofa very slowly so as not to scare the thing. I was completely focused on my work.

'I can't see anything,' I said after about ten minutes. 'Perhaps it has found a way into the frame.'

I huffed as I stood and was about to explain to her that we could either dismantle her furniture or wait until it reappeared when I realized she was completely naked and I had been well and truly set up. She raised her hand dramatically and exclaimed: 'Stop! I am your spider.'

Then she leaned over to a CD player on a table and pressed play. The opening bars of 'The Stripper' issued from the speakers. Ta-dah, dah, dah! The woman sauntered over to me, pushed me down onto the sofa and performed a well-practised dance routine, the finale of which involved a lollipop which she produced from somewhere lollipops aren't meant to go. When the music finished Jim and Phil sang 'Happy Birthday'.

Life often went from the sublime to the ridiculous, or back the other way. The fake spider was dramatic in its own bizarre way but we were experiencing plenty of real-life drama that was making the series extremely popular. At its peak it had around 5 million viewers. I received a commendation from the RSPCA for one rescue, mainly because they were too bound up by health and safety rules to attempt it themselves. They called me in after a duck got stranded in the middle of a frozen lake in Reigate, Surrey. The duck had become wrapped in a fishing line and couldn't swim away. It was struggling in the cold water. It had been a particularly cold winter in the south-east with record-breaking sub-zero temperatures, and most lakes and ponds were covered in thick ice. We were called out to several weather related emergencies that year and no matter how much I padded myself out with thick coats and gloves, I still felt the cold. At home I set the heating to 26°C as a rule and even in the height of the summer it is not unusual to find me in my office with a portable radiator switched on by my desk. As you can imagine, that winter was not my favourite time of year. The thing that kept me motivated on that particular rescue – apart from the overriding urge to save the animal – was the knowledge that the café in the park where the lake was situated supplied a rather good bacon-and-egg sandwich.

The call came in and I grabbed one of the volunteers who was on duty at the centre and we loaded the Volvo with the equipment I thought we might need: ladders, the boat, a grabber, rope. When we arrived we drove into the park and got as near to the lake as we could, where we were met by two slightly apologetic RSPCA officers who explained that the duck had been spotted by a member of the public and had been stranded for at least three hours. The temperature was dropping and the lake had frozen around the bird. If no one saved it, it risked being entombed in an icy grave. It was at least 100 metres from the bank and it would have been far too risky to try and walk out to it so we unloaded the rigid fibreglass boat from the roof rack, attached a rope to the boat from a tree and, using a pickaxe, broke an area in the ice big enough to drop the boat into. We then both clambered aboard. Neither of us wore lifejackets but I figured if the boat capsized hypothermia would get us before we drowned. We inched forward into the middle of the water, using the axe to break a path for the boat. It took ages to break through every bit of thick ice to get to the duck. It was obvious the bird was in a bad way; it was cold and exhausted and occasionally flapped weakly as we approached. I tried to take it as carefully as I could because I didn't want to panic it any more than it already was but I was also very aware that time was of the essence. I was completely focused on the duck and didn't think about my own safety, even though I couldn't feel my hands. To his credit the volunteer didn't think about his safety either and we managed to get near enough to the duck for me to lean precariously over the side and carefully untangle it. I lifted it into the boat where I wrapped it in a towel and then we used the rope to pull ourselves back to shore. We took the duck back to the centre where it warmed up and was released a few days later.

Several months later I received notice from the RSPCA that I had been awarded a Certificate of Commendation for the rescue. I didn't chase awards and I did what I did for the animals not the glory, but I'd be lying if I said it wasn't nice to know that others appreciated my work – not that I saw it as work. Rescuing had never been a job: it was my calling and I lived and breathed Wildlife Aid – it was me, it was my heart and soul, it was the first thing I thought about in the morning and the last thing I thought about at night. I started work sometimes at 4.30 in the morning and loved getting up early because I could get more done when no one was around. I finished at around nine in the evening and was on call most nights. The centre and Randalls Farm was my kingdom and my castle. I hated being away from it for any length of time, and was blindly devoted to it, which made my personal life complicated. I suspect that some of my girlfriends liked the idea of dating someone who led the kind of life I did. Initially, it probably seemed romantic and exciting. And I was always honest with them.

'I do it 24/7. It comes first,' I explained to each one.

And perhaps they thought, *Great, that's really sweet, but I'll be able to change him.* Then eventually they would realize that they couldn't change me, and that I really did work 24/7. They got fed up because we would never go out and never go away anywhere. After Jill, I had several long-term relationships but they had to be on my terms, which were far too difficult for most people. My devotion to the charity was hard to accept and it was very unfair on my girlfriends. However, I enjoyed the chase and in 2007 I set my sights on a tall, blonde, attractive woman, several years younger than me.

I love tapas and there was a restaurant near the centre that the crew and I would often frequent after a long day. I noticed a new member of staff there one day and was immediately drawn to her. She was stunning, friendly and, thankfully, wasn't offended by my jokey chat-up lines. Her name was Stanislava, Stani for short. She was Slovakian and over the following months I made it my mission to win her over. Initially, she probably thought I was a pest but I persevered. I'm a big believer in the philosophy that if you try hard enough you can achieve anything in life so the tapas became a weekly treat. I must have spent thousands in the restaurant because it took a year before she agreed to go on a date with me, and even then she called just beforehand to ask, 'It is only as friends, isn't it?'

We got on well and one date turned into another until she eventually came to live with me. Like most things in my life, it just sort of happened. She came for a couple of nights and over time stayed longer. The first time she came back to Randalls was for a drink after work and she brought in a pizza. At the time I had a flat-coated retriever called Bear, who grabbed her by the arm with his mouth and walked her in. Stani was terrified – she didn't know if he was going to kill her or take her arm off. He was very gentle, though, and had simply smelled the pizza. She gave him some and he loved her for evermore. She became involved in the centre and in my life gradually. For quite a few years she didn't have much to do with the animals but over the years she became really good with our badgers and she can now get some badger cubs to feed that no one else can. She will feed them every two hours through the night, which takes both patience and commitment. We all have our own fields of expertise. Mine is managing to look incredibly busy and knowledgeable whereas actually I do nothing and know nothing!

Stani takes no crap and tells it straight, which works well for me because I need someone fiery. I can be quite domineering and I like getting my own way so I need a strong woman to stand up to me, and sadly a lot of the people I've known haven't. Stani tells me in no uncertain terms what to do if I try and take the piss.

The Zambia special went down a treat with the broadcaster and also gave me the impetus to consider other locations. It took a lot to drag me away from the centre and from my work but we all realized that the international dimension gave the show a fresh new direction. The format for the international trips needed to mirror the content of the domestic shows. We needed to feature people who did in other countries what I did in the UK; we needed to shadow them, feature their dramatic rescues and releases, and also raise awareness of the conservation and environmental problems they were facing in their own countries. We began by drawing up a list of locations. They needed to be exotic enough to make good television.

'How about the Arctic?' Jason suggested.

'Too cold,' I answered.

'India?'

'Too much dysentery,' I mused.

For the following six years the crew repeatedly tried to get me to go to India but I always put a veto on it. It was just too hot, busy, dirty and manic for me. Jim and I would always disagree about where we were going because I didn't want to go on some of the trips at all. I threw my toys out the pram and got stroppy. He ignored me and arranged them anyway. He has a brilliant eye for what makes good television and gently pushed me past my comfort zone to make the series better.

'It should be in the southern hemisphere,' I suggested, 'and we'll go when its winter here.' We all liked the idea of getting a week in the sun when the weather was grotty at home but it also made sense. Although winter provided dramatic and atmospheric rescue footage for the show, it was also our quiet period so the trips would give us a better range of content. We planned a timetable; each winter we would try and squeeze in one or two international trips, which we could then edit into several specials that would be broadcast throughout a series run.

'And I have to travel business class,' I explained. I had suffered from a bad back for many years and there was a danger that a long-haul flight in cattle class would leave me laid up and unable to film. The others raised their eyebrows but I convinced them that business-class flights for me were an insurance policy worth paying. The whole trip would be a waste of time and money if I were unable to film through injury or illness – well, that was my story anyway!

The first trip after Zambia saw the team and me back on familiar territory on the African continent at the rescue centre in South Africa we had visited briefly during the Zambia trip. The Centre for Rehabilitation of Wildlife (CROW) was run by Dr Helena Fitchat, who is half-Czech and married to a South African farmer. She is a real character who has devoted her life to rescuing wildlife. The centre is a parallel version of Wildlife Aid; we have badgers and hedgehogs, while they have baboons and warthogs. On our first trip there we filmed a couple of lion cubs Helena was rearing. They had been confiscated from a notorious poacher who had taken them from the wild in order to sell them into the cruel 'canned hunting' industry – the shameful business in which captive wild animals are raised and then released into a controlled environment where trophy hunters pay to shoot them. At the time, there were thought to be around 5,000 lions in captive breeding programmes supplying this completely legal but deeply immoral business. The animals do not get a chance: they are released into penned-off areas, sometimes sedated and then lured out into open where they make easy targets for cowardly hunters who shoot them from the safety of vehicles. Often the hunters are poor shots and the animals die slow and agonizing deaths. I found this whole practice abhorrent. Helena called us out of blue and explained that the lion cubs we had filmed on the first visit were being transferred to a conservation programme that aimed to train them to survive in the wild. She wanted us to film the story and even paid for the flights, so we could hardly refuse.

After a long journey we drove to her centre where she showed us the lions which, in the interim, had grown into stunning adolescents. The male wasn't fully grown but was already incredibly powerful and muscular. The previous year I had gone in the pen with it. Now it was far too large to risk getting close to. The fate of the lions had remained in doubt after our first visit because Helena shared the same ethos as me: that it was kinder to euthanize a wild animal that couldn't go back in the wild, rather than keep it in the hell of captivity. Many conservationists in South Africa believed that it was impossible to rehabilitate captive-bred lions or frankly didn't want to take the risk on such big, dangerous animals. However, Helena had found an enormous private game sanctuary that was willing to take the lions and give them the specialist training they needed to be wild again.

I wanted to use the opportunity to highlight the canned hunting industry and so before we left we got in touch with a 'lion farmer' who bred lions to supply the hunting market and arranged to interview him. It was a tough call for me. His line of work was sickening but was legal in his country. In order to expose the cruelty of the practice I needed to gain his trust. I wanted him to be open and honest with me so I couldn't blunder in and be critical or judgemental. We drove six hours to his 'farm' where he bred a large number of big cats and also rare white lions.

He showed us around and explained that his lions were sold to zoos, sometimes exported abroad, and that some were hunted. He admitted that he didn't know what fates awaited the animals he sold. He fed them dead cattle and old horses. He explained that some lions were set free in small parks where hunters could track them for an authentic adventure but also admitted that in other places lions were lured into exposed areas with meat tied to trees. He said he wasn't involved in canned hunting and that the lions he bred were only hunted over large areas and not lured. It was a moot point as far as I was concerned. Hunting animals for sport was not something with which I agreed. He tried to excuse himself by claiming that, by breeding lions, he was helping conserve the species in case it went into decline. At £10,000 a lion I could understand why he wanted to protect his business with a conservation smokescreen. He let us film one of his adorable cubs, which I found extremely difficult, knowing that in two years' time it was destined either for a foreign zoo or a hunter's bullet. Canned hunting continues and even if the South African government bans it, it will be impossible to enforce a ban in such a huge nation with remote regions. The only way it will stop is when all governments ban the importation of hunting trophies – the mounted evidence taken home after a successful hunt. Without trophies, hunters are less likely to spend their money killing animals.

Helena's lions were lucky: they escaped the trade. We followed them as they were transferred to a wonderful reserve where conservationists and scientists had created a natural ecosystem so they could study a huge range of wildlife behaviour.

There were many similarities between CROW and Wildlife Aid. Many of the patients Helena saw had come to grief as a result of urban encroachment – road accidents were a common problem. Once they had recovered, she released them back into the wild just as we did. Before we left CROW Helen explained there was one last thing to film which would make engaging content.

'Feeding time with the Cape gannets,' she said.

Cape gannets are seabirds that plunge into the water and dive for the fish and CROW had two of them in an enclosure.

'You go in first and feed the gannets by hand. Hold out a fish and they will take it,' Jim said to me. 'We'll follow you in and get the shot from behind.'

I knew exactly what was going on when I was given a bowl of fish. Jim and Helena thought it would be funny to see me tackling the birds, which are voracious peckers with sharp bills. Unbeknown to the crew, I'd had gannets in Leatherhead before and I knew they would have a go at me. They also forgot that they were all wearing flip-flops and T-shirts while I wore boots and a shirt. I walked in the enclosure first and sure enough the gannets came over once they saw the fish but I was experienced enough to dodge them and take control of the situation. When Phil, Jim and Jason followed the gannets saw their toes, thought they were food and went for them, drawing blood in the process.

While we worked hard on the trips, which were often stressful, we also tried to have fun and often played practical jokes on each other. One night in South Africa we were staying at a reserve when there was a spectacular thunderstorm.

'This will make an excellent moody shot,' Jim and Phil explained in unison. They encouraged me to stand in the rain on a veranda and laughed at my reaction, probably hoping for some dramatic shots of me being struck by a lightning bolt! On another occasion we were travelling through mountainous coastal terrain and Jim spotted a cave in a cliff wall below the road. He decided it would make a spectacular 'general view' (GV).

'We could shoot from the cave and get the sea beyond in the background,' he said.

I am not comfortable with heights so while they managed to negotiate the narrow, precarious path down to the cave with the equipment I struggled and inched along it, clinging on to the cliff face. I was hanging on for dear life at points, hugging the rock wall and cursing. By the time I got to the relative safety of the cave I was terrified and panicking in the knowledge that I had to do the journey over again to get back to the car.

Generally, I tried to look after myself when we travelled. The boys often enjoyed a drink after a day's work. I couldn't afford to be off my game, however, because I had to anchor the show. I even watched what I ate and when we were in more remote places would survive off rice and vegetables for fear of being struck down with food poisoning.

At one restaurant where we stopped for lunch on the way to a location, the boys thought they'd play a trick on me. They found the hottest chilli they could and poked it inside one of the profiteroles I was having for dessert. I bit into it and realized straight away what they were up to but didn't let on and ate the rest of it. I could see them glance at each other as they carried on their conversation. I kept quiet and acted normally until we were about an hour into our journey. Then I started clearing my throat and coughing.

'I don't feel too great,' I spluttered. 'It's weird. I feel like I've eaten a chilli and I'm allergic to them.'

The boys shifted uncomfortably.

'What do you mean?' asked Jim.

'I get anaphylactic shock if I eat chillies. My throat swells up. It's serious. I could die.'

I continued coughing and lay down across the back seat of the people carrier, stringing the panic out for another hour. I could see how concerned they were; they thought they'd killed me but the bloody cowards didn't say a word! I only told them that I'd tricked them several weeks later.

During our time in South Africa we also fitted in several other assignments. I went to a sugar plantation to look at how the industry in which I had started my working life had affected wildlife. We got several episodes from the South Africa trip. The viewers were happy, the broadcasters were happy and we were happy.

Unfortunately, our globetrotting didn't go down so well back at Wildlife Aid where some people felt it was taking time away from our core mission of saving British wildlife. It was a quandary for me as I was devoted to the charity without question and hated leaving the centre, but I loved the experience and realized that the series played an important role in spreading the conservation message further afield.

Soon after returning from South Africa we had another successful multi-location trip to Australia where we made four programmes and ended up staying for a month. We lined up several stories before we went and made arrangements to meet a range of rescuers. The boys got bored on long flights and spent most of the time messing around or drinking. On the last leg to Australia they managed to get upgraded and came and sat with me in business where they availed themselves of the free champagne. Jim fell asleep in his half-reclined seat with a full champagne glass resting upright on his chest. Jason reached over and pressed the button to recline the seat fully, tipping the whole glass over Jim's face.

One of our content strands in Australia focused on kangaroos, which are hunted and eaten. We went on a kangaroo shoot one night to see what happened and to highlight the issue in much the same way we had highlighted the canned hunting story. It was not cute and cuddly but increasingly I wanted our trips abroad to show the problems facing animals everywhere. We went to a processing plant to see if the kangaroos were humanely killed and met someone who rehabilitated injured kangaroos.

While we were in Australia we chartered our own plane, which sounds ostentatious but was the most cost-effective way to get between locations because the distances were so vast. We had a pilot named Ralph and I also did some of the flying. At the time the country experienced some of the worst bush fires in its history. We were nearing the end of a six-hour flight one day when we flew straight into the path of a sandstorm that had been whipped up by the heat of the fires. I was at the controls, bringing us in to land, when I saw a huge wall of dust and debris in front of us at about 2.5 kilometres. The small plane was being buffeted around by the thermals and updraft and I gratefully handed the controls to Ralph who was the more experienced pilot. Still, he had to battle to get the plane down and we hit the runway at an angle because the crosswind was so fierce. It was a nail-biting landing and I have never been so glad to get back down on terra firma. We took amazing footage of the aftermath of the fires and captured the stories of some of the animals affected by them.

I faced my fear of snakes while in Australia. At Wildlife Aid, we have looked after five or six adders over the years plus a few escaped 'exotics' such as pythons and corn snakes. On a snake rescue my heart always goes a little faster. I deal with it but I don't enjoy them. We get a lot of slow worms, which are fine as you can just pick them up. They exude a garlic smell that stays on your hands for days. Grass snakes are fine too as they play dead when you pick them up. In Australia, I picked up a copperhead, which is the fourth most dangerous snake in the world. I would rather not have handled it but it made good TV so I watched the chap I was with do it and copied him. When

I was in overseas centres dealing with animals I was not used to, I was always guided by the local staff. After a few trips I learned that some were better than others and some were useless, and that worried me.

CHAPTER FIFTEEN

Gorillas and Militias

LIKE MILLIONS OF other people around the world I remember watching the iconic footage of David Attenborough interacting with mountain gorillas in Rwanda. The scene from the series *Life on Earth* was broadcast in 1979 and saw a young Sir David became a plaything for a young gorilla. I watched it in awe, thinking to myself, *I'll never be able to do that*. Nowadays I don't think Sir David would have been so hands-on with the animals. Conservation has moved on and we've become more educated.

I have always loved Attenborough, who has done a huge amount in shaping the nation's understanding of the natural world while maintaining his own integrity. Few people have the gravitas of Attenborough and he doesn't exploit the animals, unlike some other presenters. Steve Irwin, for example, did a lot for conservation before his death in 2006 but I did not agree with many of his methods. What happened to him was tragic, of course, but no matter how talented or loved he was, he held his kid over a crocodile for a photo opportunity. That's just stupid. And he wrestled animals for the cameras. Do we really want children to think it is okay to grab a crocodile? If an animal is sick, I will get it; if it's not, I will leave it. I won't just pick it up to amuse the audience. I have tried hard not to use wildlife as entertainment and I think that is the ethos that David Attenborough follows, too.

We had a very good commissioning editor through much of our time at the Discovery channel who understood what we were trying to achieve and who let us get on with it. However, commercial television is all about profit and audience share. There are no broadcasters doing it purely for ethical reasons. They are making or buying in programmes with the sole aim of getting their ratings up. The media have a great opportunity to drive home the message of conservation and environmentalism but largely they don't take it; the media play to the lowest common denominator because that's where the profits are. It is a shame because I believe people are more discerning and would watch things with more depth and authenticity.

I have no idea why *SOS* was successful; it was just me doing what I do but people liked it and I thank every viewer. It gave me the opportunity to do some amazing things and see things I would never have seen. Which brings us back to gorillas.

As we scoured the globe for potential expedition ideas the mountain gorillas were a constant draw. It was initially

Jim's idea, although I wasn't averse because I had always wanted to see them.

With a bit of research, we found an American charity called the Mountain Gorilla Veterinary Project, or the Gorilla Doctors as they are also known. They monitor the gorillas in the vast Virunga National Park. The 7,800-square-kilometre park is situated in the Democratic Republic of Congo (DR Congo), which despite its name isn't particularly democratic. A five-year conflict at the turn of the century pitted government forces, supported by Angola, Namibia and Zimbabwe, against rebels backed by Uganda and Rwanda. Despite a peace deal and the formation of a transitional government in 2003, people in the east of the country, where Virunga is, remained in fear of death, rape or displacement by marauding militias and the army. The war claimed up to 6 million lives, either as a direct result of fighting or because of disease and malnutrition. The UK Foreign Office advised against travel to the region. The more we researched, the more I realized the trip was well outside my comfort zone and, while I wanted to go, I was very apprehensive. So was Lou who gave Jim a particularly hard time, telling him, 'Just remember Dad's a sixty-year-old man. If he dies, you are dead.'

However, I had a lot of confidence in the Gorilla Doctors, whose headquarters are in neighbouring Rwanda. They could not guarantee safety in such a volatile environment but they knew how to mitigate risks. After several months of careful planning we flew to Rwanda to meet them.

The Gorilla Doctors are made up of a multinational team

of vets, conservationists and local guides whose mission is to protect the gorillas and keep them healthy until they become a self-sustaining population. They are among the most endangered primates on the planet and face risks from loss of habitat, poachers and disease. Sometimes they wander into neighbouring villages and the Doctors are called to rescue them and take them back to the safety of the remote part of the park in which they live.

Our flight to Rwanda was unremarkable except for some high jinks from the boys during which Jason managed to get a life vest over Jim, who had fallen asleep as usual. Jason pulled the toggle to inflate the vest. Jim woke up startled as his colleague shone the light from his phone in his face and screamed 'We're going down.' The boys got a huge bollocking from the cabin staff and, when I heard about the episode, I silently thanked God that I had travelled in another part of the plane, but I did laugh out loud.

I was pleasantly surprised when we landed in Rwanda. Given its history of genocide and conflict, it was surprisingly tranquil and had a reasonable infrastructure. We drove to the Gorilla Doctors HQ where we filmed some interviews and then made our way out of Rwanda and into DR Congo. Our destination was the town of Goma (FO advice: only travel there if essential). We crossed over the border and it was like travelling back 100 years. The border crossing was nothing more than an old shack and the guards were brooding and aggressive, not the kind of people you could have a laugh with. They emptied our bags and equipment, searching through everything silently and looking over all our documentation in intimidating detail. Goma was only 100 metres over the border but the roads were tracks littered with potholes that were more than a metre deep in places. There didn't seem to be any manmade surfaces anywhere, just mud, dust and dirt. At one stage I looked out the 4x4 window and saw a child fall into an open sewer.

The place felt tense and very unstable. It was not unusual for gun battles to break out between rival factions and the slightest incident could spark demonstrations and violence. There were hardly any goods in the shops and what little there was, was out of date. No one wanted to deal in the local currency because it was effectively worthless and the slightest political problem sent its value crashing even further so everyone wanted dollars. Before we had left the UK I knew the experience was going to be dodgy but it never dawned on me just how dodgy until I was there.

The first night we went into Goma it was like entering anarchy. We stayed in a seedy hotel, which was one of the best in the town, and we had our own security detail to look after us because of the risks to foreigners. I lay in bed that night, nervously listening to the noises outside, wondering whether the bangs in the distance were gunfire. Outside my door sat a man with an AK47 on his lap to make sure I was okay.

I live in Surrey for Christ's sake, I thought to myself. I realized what a very sheltered, blessed life I had. People in the UK who think they have a bad lot in life need to go out to Goma and get a reality check.

After a restless night, we were very glad to get out of town and headed up into the Virunga National Park, which is a protected UNESCO site that has many of the world's most endangered species within it, plus a lot of insurgents coming in and wrecking everything. It is an ark in the middle of a sea of human crap and the park is run by a chap for whom I have more respect than possibly anyone else I have ever met. I only learned when I got back home that Emmanuel de Merode is a Belgian prince because he made nothing of it and has devoted his life to running the park and protecting the animals in it. He has a team of rangers trying to protect the animals from illegal loggers, charcoal burners, poachers and militias. Each year around twenty of the rangers are killed. I spent time chatting with him and he was softly spoken and incredibly nice. If I was a Belgian prince would I be doing what he does? Would I hell! Some years after the trip he was shot in a raid and wounded through his lungs and stomach. He was in hospital for two weeks and went straight back to the park when he got out. He is a tough man.

We stayed in Emmanuel's camp, which was the staging post for most trips to see the gorillas. Access to them was very carefully controlled. From the camp it was a half-day guided hike up steep mountains to the gorillas. Although there wasn't much security inside the camp there were watchtowers with armed guards at each corner. Before we left in the morning we were given a briefing by the guides who were accompanying us. Interaction between man and gorilla needed to be kept to a minimum, for our safety and for the gorillas. We were told not to stare at them directly, to look away if they looked at us and not to stand directly in front of them. It was also forbidden to smoke and we were told not to wear deodorant as they had an acute sense of smell. The guides explained that they would tell us exactly what to do once we were near the apes.

Soon after we set off I started to struggle. I hadn't realized that we were high up to start with and from our base we went up further along the slopes of an inactive volcano. I had made no allowances for the altitude and the thin air, and hadn't had any time to acclimatize. It was probably a good thing I wasn't allowed to smoke because before long I was puffing. It was a steep slog through dense undergrowth. The guides went in front to cut a path with their machetes. They were expert trackers who knew the terrain intimately and could locate the gorillas by their tracks. About halfway, one of the vets with us, Dr Jan Ramer, turned to Jason.

'Is Simon okay? He is looking very green. Is he going to die?' she asked.

I was leaning against a tree wheezing. I gestured that I would be okay in a few minutes after I'd caught my breath.

Jim had our big broadcast camera, which weighed about 11 kilograms, plus spare batteries and tapes. He managed to get that up while I struggled to get myself up. After a couple of hours it started to rain, which made walking even more difficult. I concentrated on taking each step, carefully trying to negotiate my way through the path that the guides had hacked away for us. The going was slow and I needed to take frequent stops. After three hours' trekking we were urged to slow down and told to put on the face masks that had been provided. These were essential because there is a zoonotic link between humans and apes, meaning they can catch germs from us and vice versa. It was a sure sign that we were close. The guides had been following tracks for about half an hour and explained that we needed to be slow and quiet in order not to startle the animals. A few metres on and they told us to stop before pointing to a clearing.

I looked through a gap in the trees and there, just a few metres in front of us, lay a juvenile gorilla, looking disinterestedly at us. The sight took my breath away. I'd seen gorillas on television countless times but nothing can ever prepare you for the first time you see the majesty of one of them in the wild, up close. I was hot, soaked and slightly queasy from the altitude and exertion but I forgot all that discomfort in an instant.

The guides moved us closer and the boys started filming. They very carefully moved around to get better angles. We were told that if the gorillas charged us we had to look away but not run. We could not interact with them in any way.

'You are not chief here. There is only one chief,' I was told ominously. The guides pointed out several other members of the family group and then the 'chief' made an appearance: the huge silverback of the group. He was magnificent. Jim was filming me and I was talking quietly to Jan. I had prepared lots of facts, which I planned to use in a piece to camera with the gorilla in the background but I forgot them all with the ape just a metre away.

'Look at the size of its head,' I kept repeating. 'It is huge.' It was stunning. He had no fear of us. He didn't try to attack us, he just looked at us as if to say, 'This is my place'. There is a soul in most animals and I got a real sense that the gorillas were benevolent, peaceful creatures struggling to live. When we went on our trip the global population of mountain gorillas was around 980 – critically low. The Gorilla Doctors were making a difference and numbers had risen but sadly people just didn't care enough and the apes remain in crisis.

We stayed with the gorillas long enough for the vets to monitor them and do routine health assessments. Jan explained that a while ago the young gorilla we were seeing had suffered pneumonia and had been darted with antibiotics.

While the park arranged tourist visits, numbers were kept to an absolute minimum – only six people were allowed up a day and were only allowed to view the gorillas for an hour.

One of the gorillas, Noel, came extremely close out of curiosity and one of the guides hit the undergrowth around him with a stick and made warning noises.

'We want to encourage them to stay away from man for their own safety,' explained Jan.

After a while the whole family group appeared from the undergrowth around us and I got the chance to see the newest member, a tiny baby, which was being held by its mother. I watched fascinated as she nursed the tiny infant.

I could have stayed for hours but eventually we outstayed our welcome and one of the silverbacks of the group came through the bushes and 'displayed'. He stood in front of us, pursing his lips. It wasn't aggressive, it was his way of telling us he was the boss and it was time for us to leave, which we did without argument.

We spent several more days in Virunga and Emmanuel took me up in a plane to show me just how vast it is. The lush landscape is dotted with volcanoes and he took me over the biggest lava lake in the world in the top of one of the park's most active peaks. We could feel the turbulence created by the heat as we passed overhead. The guides also showed me just how prevalent poaching is. They had a warehouse full of traps that had been discovered over the years.

I almost forgot just how volatile DR Congo was after spending time with inspirational people like Emmanuel, Jan and the rangers, but we got a reminder on the way back to the relative safety of Rwanda. We drove the long way round to get some more shots for the episode and were on dirt roads for most of the way. The signposts we passed were peppered with bullet holes left over from previous skirmishes. There were three guides with us who appeared increasingly twitchy as the five-hour journey went on. They were talking to each other nervously and, as I couldn't understand them, I didn't know why. They kept stopping the car and going into farms. After several stops one of the men came back with a 23-litre drum of diesel, which a farmer had sold him. We had been low on fuel and it wasn't until we got back to the safety of a hotel that night that the guide told us if we had broken down on the road we were on with no diesel we wouldn't have been alive in the morning.

Africa provided a rich source of stories for us. On another trip we ventured to Namibia where we filmed a cheetah conservationist, Dr Laurie Marker. She had been running the Cheetah Conservation Fund there for over twenty years and remains one of the world's top cheetah experts.

We filmed remarkable footage of the animals hunting and had only been there a day when one of the sixty-two animals she looked after was injured in an encounter with a large, possibly rabid, antelope that had broken into an enclosure. The poor cheetah, Chewbacca, was one of her oldest, and was unconscious and covered in bruises. She had rescued him when he was just a few weeks old and had been caught in a trap. Sadly, he died from his injuries.

When we were filming the big cats in the wild we were told not to run at any time – which seemed like common sense given the fact that we were unlikely to be able to outrun the fastest animal on earth. One of the crew, however, who will remain nameless, lost his bottle during one shoot and legged it back to the vehicle, which aroused considerable interest from the cheetah we were observing. It suddenly thought lunchtime had arrived, stood up and looked over at us. Being the good boss I am I let the other crew back away first while I stood there in the open thinking, *I really don't want to be here at all.* Every instinct told me to turn and run and it took all my willpower to follow the advice and walk quietly back to the vehicle. That moment made the drink at the end of the day that little bit more refreshing.

Laurie is passionate about her cheetahs and explained their plight. When she moved from the USA to Namibia to set up her project, cheetahs were being killed like flies by hunters. She explained that cheetahs predated on domestic goat herds so there was constant conflict between the big cats and the goat farmers who would shoot the cheetahs to protect their herds. In order to break this cycle of conflict she had come up with a clever idea and trained dogs to protect goat herds from the cheetahs. She then gave the guard dogs to the farmers. The predators would rather go for wild game than risk being injured by a dog for an easy meal.

In one sequence we filmed, Laurie was explaining all this in a pen of goats to illustrate the point and I got the giggles. She explained that there was a war going on between cheetahs and goats, which placed an image in my head of goats and cheetahs with tanks and guns attacking each other. While I was trying to suppress the giggles, I lost my train of thought and started to make a bizarre analogy about fruit puddings. I could see Jim looking at me blankly while Laurie looked at me like I was mad.

'There is nothing faster on the planet than a cheetah,' she explained.

'What about a Lamborghini?' Jim said from behind the camera, which made us laugh even more. The more serious she was being, the harder I found it not to laugh. To top it all off one of the goats chewed through the cable on Jim's earphone. It was a hugely rewarding trip and, despite my appalling giggles, I left Namibia feeling a close kinship with Laurie and the work she was doing.

CHAPTER SIXTEEN

Undercover in the Temple

THE DEVOTION TO wildlife and conservation that I encountered over the years, from people like Laurie and Emmanuel to the volunteers and fundraisers at Wildlife Aid, has been remarkable. Wildlife Aid only grew because of the work and generosity of the people who gave their time, resources and money. All these people have been kindred spirits and we are all bound by a common purpose and mutual respect. Some of the efforts people have gone to to make sure Wildlife Aid survives have been phenomenal. One volunteer, Morven Panton, even swam the Channel to raise funds for us. I went with her on a boat as support and, let me tell you, I wouldn't go through what she went through for anyone. It was a long, cold slog for me and I was on the boat. Heaven knows what it was like for her in the water, battling currents and getting stung by jellyfish on the way. The most disheartening thing was that after a long swim in the dark we sighted land and thought, *Thank God, we're almost there*, but it was still another five hours before she made landfall because the tide was against her. She raised several thousands of pounds for us and became the youngest ever swimmer to cross the Channel when she did it in 1995.

Wildlife Aid relied on volunteers in its infancy and still does. For many years we had no paid staff at all but, as we grew, we employed people to make sure the charity ran as effectively as possibly. We have an office manager, Becky, who joined in 2006, a full-time vet nurse and also a full-time vet. Lou also came to work for us and is now Deputy CEO. Our first vet nurse, Sara, stayed with us for eight years and after she left we advertised for a replacement. Like all the adverts we have ever placed we hardly had any replies but one was perfect. Lucy came for a job interview and she'd taken a little Dutch courage before she arrived. She admitted that she had watched all the *SOS* shows and loved our work. She was so nervous about meeting me that she had a quick drink beforehand to steady her nerves. I liked her immediately and tried to dissuade her from joining, just as I did with everyone.

'It is damn tough. It's not nine to five, it's nine to whenever. You work weekends and long hours. It will take over your life and I will ask more and more of you,' I explained. She wasn't perturbed.

'You'll also be filmed,' I continued. 'You will have to come out on rescues and look after all the volunteers.'

She nodded and asked: 'When can I start?'

Lucy turned out to be a godsend and her addition to the Wildlife Aid family meant I could go on filming trips with plenty of confidence that things were being looked after back at the centre.

In series ten of *Wildlife SOS* we headed out to Thailand and Vietnam in South-east Asia with the aim of documenting some of the extremely cruel practices that were taking place in that part of the world. As in previous expeditions we hooked up with local campaigners, conservationists and activists. In Thailand, we met a man named Edwin Wiek, a Dutch expat with a military background who founded Wildlife Friends Foundation Thailand (WFFT), an organization that rescues and rehabilitates everything from gibbons to elephants. WFFT is extremely busy, mainly because attitudes to animal welfare across large parts of Thailand are lax to say the least. Edwin has been a constant thorn in the side of the authorities, which either ignore cruelty, poaching and the illegal exportation of endangered animals or, in some cases, take backhanders to turn a blind eye. He has been thrown in jail for his troubles on several occasions.

Like Wildlife Aid, Edwin and his volunteers rescue animals. Often they are called in to look after wildlife that has been injured after coming into contact with man or take in animals that have been confiscated by those in authority who do care. Many of these confiscated animals are humanized and unable to go back in the wild so WFFT runs centres where permanent residents are homed and which are part-funded by paid visitors. In essence they are zoos, which I don't agree with, but it is different stokes for different folks and in different countries you have different situations. We are lucky in the UK because most of the animals we see came straight in from the wild and we can release them back knowing they would stand a good chance of survival. However, the sort of exotic wildlife Edwin and other international rescuers deal with have often been captive for years and also stand the risk of being caught again in the wild. Edwin's centres provide a better life for the animals homed there but it is still not the utopia I'd like to see.

He took us on a monkey rescue to farmland in a rural suburb outside Bangkok. WFFT had received a tip off that a man was keeping a monkey in a cage. Sadly, it is a common occurrence. People would buy baby monkeys as pets for their children on the black market and keep them in awful conditions, usually outside in cages. The children would become bored of the animals, which are chucked a bit of food now and then and never let out. The animals would become aggressive but the owners, who are not educated about animal welfare, would not want to get rid of them because they paid money for them in the first place. Edwin was a negotiator. He would have to go to the houses and speak to the owners and convince them calmly and politely that the animals shouldn't be there. Sometimes the owners demanded compensation. He is very good at what he does and has freed animals from the most awful situations – some had been in cages for decades.

The monkey we accompanied him to rescue was locked in a small, dilapidated cage with rusty bars and no room to climb or move around in and no enrichment toys for stimulation. The poor thing was languid and bored beyond belief with dull eyes and no muscle tone. It was just wasting away with only a scrubby bit of wasteland to look at. Edwin spoke at length to the owner with consummate diplomacy and negotiated its release. Following the rescue, we went to a remote sanctuary where the charity looks after its animals. On the way we witnessed the effects of logging and deforestation and drove through beautiful woodland to the edge of a treeline beyond which huge swathes of forest had been chopped down, leaving a barren, lifeless landscape of stumps. Everything was dead. The habitat had been destroyed.

We stayed a few days in the jungle to film at the centre. There was only a rundown hostel and it was so bad even Jim, who could normally stomach a high degree of discomfort, recoiled when he saw the rooms. The bedsheets were damp, there were cockroaches everywhere and you couldn't even use the bathroom because it smelled so strongly of effluent. There was a communal area where you could eat but the food was covered in flies and looked horrendous. We were taken to a restaurant at the top of a mountain where they had all these awful-looking dishes with chickens' feet and beaks mixed in. Jim and Jason joined the locals and ate native. I took one look and ordered spinach and rice. Jim and Jason were sick as dogs for two days afterwards.

Back in the relative civilization of the city we plotted one of our most difficult assignments to date: an undercover visit to one of Bangkok's most notorious animal attractions, an animal prison called Pata Zoo. The horrific tourist attraction was an indoor menagerie of 200 captive animals confined in concrete enclosures in the upper two floors of the Pata department store in the bustling Bang Phlat commercial district. A gorilla, a tiger and penguins were held in cages and forced to perform tricks, and monkeys and apes were trained to fire-juggle, perform in costumes and take part in mock fights with keepers.

The store owners had been pressured by animal rights campaigners for many years and as a result filming was forbidden. Every now and then rumours surfaced that the animals were going to be freed but it never happened and the owners always maintained that they loved the animals and that they were well looked after. Edwin was banned, having been one of the most vocal opponents. Security was tight and there was no way we would be allowed to film inside the zoo if we went through the official channels and submitted a request to the store management. We needed to film undercover so we hid cameras in hold-alls in which we cut holes for the lenses. Edwin drove us and waited outside in the car. The four of us went in and split up into pairs so as not to arouse suspicion.

I don't mind admitting that I was incredibly nervous. Before we went in we talked through as much as we could. We knew from research and from speaking to Edwin that there was a gorilla and a tiger inside, but it was hard to know exactly what we were going to see. For such a notorious attraction, there was very little fanfare or advertising at the entrance. The whole place was dank, hot and oppressive.

Everything was grey concrete or rusty iron. Every now and then an effort had been made to brighten things up with plastic foliage but that just added to the depressing feeling of the place. The animals were in tiny dark enclosures. Each one I passed filled me with horror so I switched into work mode and started trying to record as much as I could. Jim quietly directed me, telling me to linger at certain pens.

'Just be yourself and say a piece to camera,' he said. I spoke quietly and fought back an urge to get out of the place. For an animal lover it was like being in the middle of a horror movie. What sickened me as much as the conditions were the reactions of the other visitors. The people loved it. Kids were pointing and laughing and no one was telling them that the animals shouldn't be there and shouldn't be performing. I don't mind parents taking children to zoos if they explain that zoos are bad and that the animals in them are suffering. What made things worse in Pata Zoo was that some of the visitors were Westerners who should have known better. I was numb.

The worst exhibits were the tiger and the gorilla. The big cat was confined in a barred enclosure about 3 metres square in which there was just an artificial rock for it to lie on. The gorilla's cell was no better and I stared into its eyes and wept. Gorillas in the wild have the most expressive eyes, but this wretched thing had nothing there. I just knew he wanted to be dead. He was imprisoned indoors with nowhere to go.

After we'd seen as much as we could stomach, Jim, who had the larger camera in his backpack and was feeling rebellious, got the equipment out and started filming in full view of everyone. He wanted to provoke a reaction and it worked. Suddenly, as if from nowhere, security guards appeared and started walking towards us. Jim managed five seconds of filming and then we quickly got out of there and beat a hasty retreat. I didn't look back and reached the ground floor as fast as I could. I thought we were going to end up in the notorious 'Bangkok Hilton' jail.

That evening we went out in the city to film an excerpt about the elephants of Bangkok. In and around the city there are several elephant trainers who charge tourists to ride and feed their animals, which are a common sight wandering around the busy, polluted streets. WFFT had been instrumental in saving many of these animals and rehoming them in a sanctuary in the countryside far away from the grim cityscape.

Thailand is home to wild Asian elephants but the population is struggling with only around 2,000 left. Historically, these had been captured and domesticated to be used mainly in the logging industry, ironically helping to destroy the very habitat they needed to survive. After a ban on logging, most of these elephants ended up being used for the tourism industry, giving rides in amusement parks or begging on the streets of big cities, walking day and night, and were often involved in horrific traffic accidents. There were no laws to prevent the abuse and mistreatment. To tame an elephant, a trainer has to break its spirit, which is a grotesque process that takes a long time and is worse than any torture I can imagine. The animals are roped together in cages, beaten with poles with 10-centimetre curved spikes on the end and have fire waved in front of them to scare them into eventual submission. Out on the streets of Bangkok it was not hard to find elephants, and tourists petting and riding them. I tried to get interviews with several Westerners who were paying for rides but no one wanted to be on camera, which suggested to me that they knew the practice was wrong and inhumane yet still supported it. What also concerned me was that many of the elephants we saw were too young to have been involved in the logging industry, which meant they had been captured in the wild or smuggled across the border from other countries.

Finally, we went on another undercover assignment to a notorious attraction. Tiger Temple, or Wat Pha Luang Ta Bua, is a Buddhist temple in western Thailand that was founded in 1994 as a forest temple and sanctuary for wild animals. It claimed to have received its first tigers legitimately in 1999 after they had been rescued from poachers. However, investigations since have suggested that rather than continuing as a rescue centre, the temple operated as a breeding facility and may have been involved in the tiger trade. It is certainly a busy tourist attraction and receives a constant stream of coach parties full of eager visitors who feed cubs and pose for photos with the animals.

Each day tigers would be put on public display so that tourists could touch and pose with them for a fee. Investigations showed that during these sessions, the tigers were given no shade, and were exposed to three hours of direct sunlight in temperatures which often rose above 40°C. Allegations against the temple were many. It was claimed the animals were mistreated to make them compliant and perform for visitors. In a report by one animal welfare organization it was observed that temple staff dragged tigers into appealing photographic positions by pulling their tails or punching and beating them. Staff also controlled the tigers by squirting tiger urine from a bottle into the animals' faces, an act of extreme aggression in tiger behaviour.

Despite the range of claims against the attraction, it was cleared of allegations of animal mistreatment in a 2015 investigation conducted by wildlife officials. Charges were pressed for unlicensed possession of thirty-eight protected birds found on the temple grounds.

I can only go on what I experienced and can assert that the whole place was vile. The tigers were chained up and, in my opinion, were drugged. I hated every second of the time I spent there. I went posing as a tourist and watched in horror as the monks displayed the tigers for baying tourists. Devoid of the compassion their religion promotes, they shamelessly exploited and tortured the animals for the benefit of tourists. There were scores of tigers – cubs and adults – brought out for the entertainment of the mob.

It is probably true that the original tigers that were taken to the temple had been rescued from poachers. The monks who accepted them probably did so with the best of intentions. But the endeavour had grown into a business and the tigers were the victims. During our time in Thailand we accompanied Edwin to another rescue at a temple. He had been tipped off about a bear kept in a cage there and when we arrived we discovered it pacing backwards and forwards in a small enclosure. It, too, had been given to the monks after being rescued from poachers and the monks genuinely loved it and had to be persuaded to let it go for a better life. But at the Tiger Temple there had been so much publicity that those in charge could have little doubt that what they were doing was regarded as cruel. It troubled me even more that the place was a temple; that religious element almost gave it moral authority in the view of the ignorant people who traipsed through its doors.

Thailand left me drained and the things I saw there disturbed me. People like Edwin do a remarkable job but I couldn't help leaving with an air of pessimism. I found it hard to believe that in the supposedly enlightened twenty-first century people still believe it is okay to go to places like Pata Zoo and Tiger Temple.

We undertook each trip with careful planning, one element of which involved our own health care. Just before one long-haul flight to an exotic location, Jim, Jason, Phil and I went to the Bupa centre in Gatwick airport for our jabs and the bill was £1,200 each. My arse felt like a pin cushion when I came out. In our bags, in addition to the over-the-counter meds, we carried industrial strength diarrhoea tablets, antibiotics and diazepam, in case I freaked out. We also took our own needles in case we needed an injection when we were away.

Soon after our trip to Thailand, we went back to South-east Asia to film in Vietnam, specifically to highlight the bear bile trade over there and the measures being taken by devoted campaigners to stamp it out.

Bear bile is used in traditional Chinese medicine and is believed to have a range of healing properties. Studies have shown that a compound contained within it, ursodeoxycholic acid, can be effective against some ailments, such as certain liver diseases. Traditional practitioners prescribe bear bile for much more, including everything from a sore throat to epilepsy. The liquid is extracted in one of the most inhumane processes on the planet. Bears are locked in medieval full-metal jackets and catheters are inserted into their stomachs to drain the bile. Most farmed bears are Asiatic black bears, commonly called moon bears because of the white crescents on their chests. They are listed as endangered by the Convention on International Trade of Exotic Species (CITES). They suffer incredible cruelty and spend their considerably long lives immobile, in agony, never seeing daylight. Depressingly, even though ursodeoxycholic acid can be cheaply synthesized in a lab, traditionalists still prefer bile milked from animals, which is often so full of impurities from infections that it is practically carcinogenic.

The practice takes place widely in Vietnam and China, and for many years one British woman has been instrumental in raising awareness and changing attitudes towards it. Jill Robinson has devoted her life to saving the bears and runs a charity called Animals Asia Foundation that rescues farmed bears and cares for them in sanctuaries. We flew to meet her in Vietnam where she was having great success getting politicians on board with her message.

Given the sensitivities of the subject and the political situation in Vietnam, which is a communist country, we were only allowed to film with a government minder in tow and were met by him in Hanoi. He was a low-ranking government official and a nice guy. I'm not sure how much he understood about our mission or who we were because one night he offered to take us to a place where the menu featured pangolin, an endangered type of scaly mammal that had been hunted to near extinction by idiots who believed it was a delicacy and that its scales had medicinal properties. We gracefully declined his offer.

From the airport he took us to the hotel that had been selected for us; I took one look and explained that I was not staying there. I didn't want to offend our guide but the place was in a dodgy part of town where I genuinely suspected that our equipment would get stolen. Thankfully, he understood and said he knew someone at the Sheraton who could get us rooms.

We took a trip out to Jill's sanctuary and filmed the work she was doing there and did some uncover work in Hanoi, covertly filming in several shops where bear bile products were on sale. Animals Asia has had the most amazing effect on the bile farming industry and has educated populations in China and Vietnam that the bile from farmed bears is more dangerous than the conditions it is supposed to treat.

With the help of Animals Asia, which is well respected, filming went without a hitch. Our minder played along and we took him out for meals and treated him as one of the crew. You have to get along because, as much as you don't agree with the ethics of what they are doing, they hold the key to getting the right footage. He loved it and had a great time.

After we had filmed at one of the sanctuaries in the countryside outside the city, one of Animals Asia's volunteers invited Jim and Jason to go swimming in a nearby waterfall. I think he liked them and they went off and climbed for hours to get to this place. When they realized they didn't have swimming stuff with them, the volunteer persuaded them to go skinny dipping. He took them to a natural rock slide and they all went down it butt naked. When they got out they were covered in leeches and the volunteer helped the boys to remove the ones that were hard to reach – all part of the service.

Jim and Jason shared a room in the hotel. One morning before we left Jason got in the shower and Jim took everything out the bedroom: the sheets, the clothes, even the phone. He brought it all to my room and left just one small face flannel. Laughing, we went downstairs to wait and see what Jason did. He came down holding the flannel over his front while his other hand covered his modesty at the back.

Both our trips to South-east Asia were a success and I felt we had filmed some strong, important footage. Sadly, things were changing at Discovery. While we continued to push to get the gritty stuff shown, the TV company showed little of it. It was clear that they weren't that interested in hard-hitting investigative reports. When it was eventually shown, I felt they had watered it down and it didn't do the animal victims justice.

CHAPTER SEVENTEEN

It Shouldn't Happen to a Wildlife Presenter

ON THE WHOLE, the people we met in centres abroad were wonderful. They were all slightly bonkers in their own way but they knew exactly what they were doing. They made my life much easier and they filled me with enough confidence to help them rescue animals I'd never encountered before. There was only one time when we lucked out, which was when we went out to Florida. The trip started badly because heavy snow in the UK delayed our departure and diverted us to New York and then Atlanta, from where we had to drive seven hours, all of which ate into our filming schedule. When we arrived in Florida I fell ill and was taken to a private doctor who filled me with drugs and injections and made my arse feel like a pin cushion once again. At least this allowed me to get to work within twenty-four hours. We were due to spend time there with a woman who ran an animal rescue centre and who had been great on the phone. She rescued a range of wildlife, from alligators to pelicans. After seeing her, we were scheduled to film segments on manatees and then fly down to Belize to meet a couple who rescued crocodiles.

We had always been careful to make sure that the people with whom we partnered were a good fit with Wildlife Aid and were comfortable on camera, but when we got to our first stop we soon realized that the lady we were shadowing came across as nervy and agitated. It got complicated because her number two was quite good so we filmed both of them, often asking the same questions to both, and made sure all the usable footage came from the deputy. We were only there for a couple of days and by the time we left the tensions were rising because the lady in charge realized what was going on. We then took a chartered seaplane to our next stop to film manatees.

It had always been one of my ambitions to encounter these incredible aquatic creatures and we visited a colony of them that lived in waters fed by warm springs. Manatees cannot survive in water less than 20°C – any cooler and they get hypothermia. The clear water our manatees lived in was a balmy 22°C; however, given my condition and the fact that I only had a wetsuit 4 mm thick, I was still freezing and shivering.

We filmed at the only place in the world where people were allowed to interact with manatees. There were very strict rules governing behaviour. It was imperative that the animals initiated the contact and, until they did, humans were required to keep a 3-metre distance. Splashing had to be kept to a minimum so as not to startle the creatures. There were cordoned-off areas all around where people could not go, which meant that the animals could bugger off whenever they wanted. Luckily, they are sociable creatures – like badgers – so they swam up and had a sniff around out of curiosity soon after I got into position. The water was only shallow and I was wearing a face mask and snorkel. A large female slowly swam towards me and all thoughts of cold went as the friendly creature slowly approached. They are beautiful animals and naturally inquisitive, which sadly means that many are injured by boats and nets. One came up to me and rolled over in the water for a scratch. As it did I saw its body was criss-crossed with scars left by jet skis or propellers.

The manatee encounter was magical but, like many of the animal stories abroad, it was bittersweet. While I was there I learned that the protected habitat in which the animals lived was threatened by development. A building company had been granted a licence to develop vast swathes of the riverfront.

In Florida, we also filmed a feature on alligators, which the crew assured me would involve a leisurely boat ride but actually resulted in me being filmed alongside one of the huge animals in the boat.

From Florida we headed to Mexico where we spent time in the jungle trying to film jaguars. We set up static cameras with night vision to try and capture footage of the elusive big cats. All we got on film were wild turkeys.

Finally, we took a long drive and headed across the border

into Belize where all our kit was confiscated by the customs officials, who offered no reason but said it would be impounded for seventy-two hours, which would have completely messed up the schedule. We travelled with an official document called a carnet, which listed all the equipment, where it had been bought and what it did. It was supposed to help clueless customs officials and usually they'd look over it and wave us through. But in Belize they started unpacking everything and made a big show of checking everything off the carnet. Luckily, I travelled with $10,000 in cash on me because I had learned that cash can get you out of tricky situations. I bunged the customs officer $1,000 and miraculously he let us and our seven big cases of kit through.

From the border we headed to the south of the country and Punta Gorda, which was home to a rescue and conservation charity run by Vince Rose and Cherie Chenot-Rose. Vince is a self-taught rescuer who studied bears in the Rocky Mountains and Saltwater crocodiles in Australia. His wife Cherie is a research biologist and reptile expert. They moved to the tiny Central American nation in 2004 to develop a large sanctuary for two species of crocodiles found in Belize – the American and Morelet's crocodiles. They built a two-storey octagonal house that rested on stilts and constructed two smaller cottages to house researchers and students. They dug out long canals for the crocodiles they rescued, bought two boats and called the place the American Crocodile Education Sanctuary.

Their dedication to the local wildlife brought them into conflict with elements of the community around them, especially the indigenous Mayans, most of whom see crocodiles as pests. Mayan children were known to take tourists to see crocs, which they lured to the riverbanks by feeding them scraps of meat. Over time the crocodiles had naturally grown to see man as a source of food and had lost their fear of humans. They had been known to attack dogs and this dangerous way for children to earn a few dollars had also led to some children being bitten. The natives also often harboured resentment of richer foreigners – which they saw Vince and Cherie as.

The crocodiles have come into increased contact with people as their habitat has been eroded by development. Often they are shot, trapped, injured and maimed, and Vince and Cherie do their best to protect them and rehabilitate them. In 2010 the tension with the community came to a head after the unrelated disappearance of two children from a town several miles away. According to news reports, a psychic who lived in the town told villagers she'd had a vision that the Roses had abducted the children and fed them to the animals at their sanctuary. This was, of course, absolute mumbo-jumbo (the missing children were safe in Guatemala, where they had been taken by their biological father). However, the superstitious Mayans believed her and a mob of angry villagers from the settlement drove to the sanctuary and torched it. Vince and Cherie, who were away at the time, received a warning from a friend that the mob was on its way and called the police, who told them they couldn't enter the property because the Roses' two dogs were barking and would not allow them in.

The fire destroyed everything they had built and the mob also killed seventeen crocodiles at the centre. I knew how devastating it was to lose everything to fire and was enraged by the senselessness of the actions of the mob.

I knew all this before I met them and I liked them immediately. We share a worldview and I admire their dogged determination in the face of the resentment they faced. Hearing their story made me realize that I was one of the fortunate ones. Back in Surrey my work was supported by the community, which was mainly wealthy. Even then fundraising was hard enough for Wildlife Aid. I couldn't imagine how hard it would be if the community was both poor and ideologically opposed to our mission. Every year Vince and Cherie struggled to stay afloat and to rebuild what they had lost. Vince had run a construction company when he lived in the US before he moved to Belize and had sunk most of his own money into building the sanctuary. Most of their fundraising had to be done back in the US because crocodiles were low down the list of financial priorities in Belize.

Their lives were constantly threatened. The locals continued to view them with suspicion and antipathy. One day Vince and I were out and we stopped at a diner to grab some lunch. I noticed something heavy in Vince's pocket and asked what it was.

'It's my .38,' he told me, matter-of-factly. I ate quickly and nervously, wondering if the people stopping in their pick-ups were coming in for food or were going to take a shot at us. I'm not sure, if I was in the same situation, I would have continued with the vocation Vince has chosen.

Vince and Cherie treat injured crocodiles and rescue ones that wander into buildings, gardens and public places. They then relocate them deeper into the mangroves and swamps that are their natural home to lessen the opportunities for contact with humans and so extend their survival rates.

Vince and Cherie have a hard life and, if I'm honest, I am not enamoured with their choice of animal to save. While I respect all wild animals, crocodiles and alligators scare me. You look into their eyes and you just know they will kill you if they get the chance, which means that I have never been comfortable around them. But Vince knows exactly what he is doing and handles them expertly. Like the best rescuers, he has an affinity with the animals and understands their behaviour. I helped him on rescues and with relocations and, under his guidance, was confident enough to handle the creatures. Crocs are big, dangerous muscular reptiles; to get one of them out of the water you need to be strong and you need to know what you are doing. I was glad Vince was there to step in if anything went awry, even though Jim did mention that my untimely death in the jaws of a crocodile would make a good season finale and boost ratings.

While crocs are dangerous, my deadliest animal encounter happened back in South Africa where I went down in a shark cage to encounter great whites.

South Africa was one of our favourite locations because it is a vast country with a diversity of wildlife and an infrastructure that allows a film crew to get around without too many problems. It was easy to stay there for a week or two and produce a variety of content. We had already filmed features on penguins and seals and, after some convincing, I was persuaded to go out with a great white shark expert and shark rescuer.

I was lulled into a false sense of security by the seal rescuer we met first. Like most rescuers he was a complete nutcase but knew exactly what he was doing. He ran a seal rescue service by himself and his rescue centre was right in the middle of a harbour where most of the fishermen hated the seals because they ate the fish. It's fair to say he wasn't too popular, but he was a tough nut and didn't care what people thought. I wouldn't have wanted to cross him on a dark night. The remarkable thing was that he never contained the seals. If they became ill, they would swim to his jetty where he would feed them and treat them. If they were too sick, they would stay there of their own accord; they were not confined in pens. They stayed because they knew they would get looked after and when they got better they left and went back out to sea. While I was there I had a go at stomach-feeding a recovering seal, which involved liquidizing fish, putting the resulting fish smoothie in a bottle, attaching a tube to the bottle and putting the other end of the tube down the seal's throat. You have to hold the tube in your mouth because you need one hand to hold the seal and one to hold the bottle. It was complicated and smelly but it was the quickest way to get food into a sick seal. It also made good footage.

Given the range of wildlife we filmed over the years it was perhaps inevitable that sooner or later I would come face to face with the apex predator of the ocean. I hate the water, especially the cold water around the Cape. I only learned how to swim when, in less enlightened times, my father adopted the literal sink or swim teaching method and threw me in the water. I trained to scuba dive but I was a reluctant swimmer and I was not very enamoured of the idea of going down in a shark cage but agreed reluctantly while secretly hoping for a last-minute cancellation due to bad weather. Unfortunately, my wish was not granted and we headed out to sea with an organization that facilitated shark dives. The guy we teamed up with was a scientist who been on TV a lot and Jim had seen all his YouTube clips. His knowledge was good but several things happened that left me questioning the safety procedures – and that's coming from me, the worst person to take any notice of health and safety.

When the deck hands loaded the shark cage up before we left I started to get slightly concerned because it looked well past its sell-by date and nothing like the ones I'd seen on television.

We left the harbour and chugged out about a kilometre to an area where there was plenty of known shark activity. Once anchored, the boat crew started to throw chum over the side. Great whites can smell the foul cocktail of decaying fish guts and blood from miles away. Thankfully, the weather was clear and sunny but the water was murky because it was the wrong time of year and the sea was choppy. The water was only about 9°C, which for me was far too cold and again I only had a thin suit because I needed to be able to move. Everyone else only had a thin suit, too, and although I had the option of a thicker one I refused because I didn't want to look like a sissy.

Jim always knew when I was nervous because I yawned a lot, and I had been yawning all morning on the boat as we made our way out. The crew assembled the cage on the deck and, in my view not awfully professionally, manhandled it over the side. Jim had hired a full face mask with a built-in radio mic at great expense. I had never worn one before and hadn't considered how to clear the air from my nose and equalize – it's a completely different technique in a full mask than in normal diving. I worked it out eventually and reluctantly climbed over the side. I dropped through the open hatch at the top of the cage into the freezing water before it was lowered into the depths where the sharks would be. I knew the boys could hear everything I was saying as I went down so I started giving a running commentary.

I didn't feel particularly confident and when my weight belt fell off I really did start to worry. I kept floating to the top of the cage and had to wedge my foot under one of the bars to keep me anchored to the bottom. Then a shark appeared and I almost wet myself. Nothing can prepare you for the sight. Suddenly, this great open mouth appeared out of the murky water heading straight towards me. It was terrifying. The shark was several metres long and so powerful it could have batted me and the cage around like a Swingball if it had so desired. The animal made several close passes and I looked into its eyes. There was nothing: they were soulless black holes.

All the while I talked incessantly and tried to describe in detail what I was seeing and feeling. What I really wanted to say was, 'Get me out of here'. I was also worried that the foot anchoring me in the cage was sticking out and would provide a toe-appetizer for my fishy friend.

I stayed down for almost an hour and the shark was joined by others. Eventually, I was relieved to feel the cage rising back through the water. Looking up, I saw the underside of the boat appear from the murk and realized that the angle of ascent was wrong. The cage was coming up at the back of the boat at a slant. It started to skew as it got closer to the surface and got stuck on the propeller at the back of the boat, where it remained dangling with me inside while the sharks circled in the gloom below. I checked my air pressure monitor and saw that I was running out of air. After several painful minutes someone topside managed to untangle the cage but in the process something bent, which meant they couldn't get the cage close enough to the boat to allow me to climb straight onto the deck. Instead, I had to swim out of the top of the cage and into the open water where the sharks were. By the time I surfaced I was so exhausted all I could do was hang on to the anchor chain and hope the sharks below didn't think I was a seal. Four people had to lift me out of the water in the most ungainly manner. They flipped me onto the boat deck like a stranded fish.

The most insane thing was that the next day we went out again and scuba dived to put back a baby shark that had been rescued. It was released on a reef just a few hundred metres from where we had encountered the big sharks in our cage the preceding day. I hadn't scuba dived for some time and, when I slipped on the jacket that regulates air, I forgot to put it on loose in order to allow it to fill out without becoming too tight as I went down. I pulled it tight and as we descended the jacket began to tighten and constrict my chest. My breaths became shallower and shallower and I struggled to breathe for much of the dive.

It was an exhausting trip and I was happy to get back to the UK where we set about editing the footage into a one-hour special. One afternoon, Jim came into the office from the editing suite.

'There's a bit of a problem with the sound on the shark dive VT,' he said frowning.

'What's wrong?' I asked.

'There's none,' he said.

'What do you mean?'

'No sound at all,' he admitted. 'The equipment didn't work.'

After spending around £1,000 hiring the special equipment it turned out to be faulty. I didn't know whether to laugh or cry.

'We need to have a commentary over it,' I exclaimed. So we came up with a plan. We redubbed the commentary from the comfort of my centrally heated office in Surrey with me talking into a walkie-talkie with a hankie over the mouthpiece to create the right effect while Jim recorded it in the next room.

CHAPTER EIGHTEEN

Over and Out

MY TRAVELS ALWAYS left me feeling conflicted. While the TV show and charity were two separate entities, they existed in a symbiotic relationship. The charity relied on the series to give it a profile we would never have been able to achieve without mass media exposure, and the series relied on the charity for content. In hindsight, however, I am not too sure that being the focus of a television series helped in terms of fundraising. I think there would have been many people who assumed that because Wildlife Aid was the subject of a fly-on-the-wall documentary, it had loads of money, which couldn't have been further from the truth.

From my point of view, I had started to understand that the series was important not just to highlight the work we did at the centre, but also to educate people and to bring to attention the wider issues facing wildlife on a global scale.

The more I saw when I went abroad, the more it became apparent that animals faced the same problem in every corner of the world – man. Pollution, over-development, over-population, selfishness and greed; the locations were different but the ingredients of the recipe for disaster were always the same. There was a global band of brothers and sisters devoting their lives to redressing the balance and rescuing man's animal victims; I tapped into this family for our international adventures but the effect they were having was minimal. What was really needed was education, so in each edited programme we sent to the channel we tried to bang home the message: the natural world is in crisis.

Knowing that there was a higher calling to the work I was doing made leaving Randalls slightly easier each time I departed on a foreign assignment. It was my counter-balance to the guilt I often felt in going away. Wildlife Aid had grown immensely. By 2010 we had over 300 volunteers and were dealing with upwards of 20,000 animal incidents a year. In that year we became a foundation, the Wildlife Aid Foundation (WAF), with a wider education remit. There was a constant stream of animals arriving in reception and the phones rang day and night with people looking for advice. On a personal level, I found it hard to leave to go filming, too. WAF was in my DNA and I believed the place needed me. I didn't like the idea that a major rescue would arise while I was away and would have to be carried out without me. I also had commitments: I had my daughters, I had Stani, I had my mother and I had my dogs.

Sam, my beloved rescue retriever, was getting old and frail. Before we went to South Africa he took a turn for the worse and I was convinced he would not be around when I returned. He couldn't move and had to be carried outside when he needed to wee. It was painful to watch and although I had made the decision to put countless animals to sleep over the years it was not a decision I could make for Sam. There was still something in his eyes that said he wanted to live. I left for the trip with a heart as heavy as lead, convinced that he would be gone by the time I returned. My instincts, however, were right and when I returned he had rallied and was still with us.

Eventually, though, like all of us, Sam succumbed to old age and died when he was seventeen, which in dog terms was a very good innings but in my eyes was too short. Sam was my soulmate and I would have happily lived another lifetime with him by my side. His death knocked me sideways and, in the same way I dealt with Dad's death, I couldn't face any ceremony after he had gone. I left that to Jim who, a few years later, told me the story of what happened to Sam. In a fitting way the tale was full of the type of dark humour that we all shared. Despite the devastation at losing him, I could still see the funny side.

Sam died at the weekend and I took his body to one of the freezers in the top barn because I couldn't leave it to decompose. I left a Post-it note on Jim's desk and went off to mourn my loss alone. Jim got in on Monday morning and saw the note.

'Sambo is in the freezer, can you take him to the pet crem?' it said.

Reluctantly Jim went up and recovered the body. He explained later that he was quite perturbed and thought poor Sam had died with a snarl on his face because rictus and the cold had pulled his lips back. Sam was big, really heavy, and he was frozen solid. Jim had to wrestle him out of the freezer and struggled to wrap his body in a blanket. His car was parked at the front of the centre so he needed to walk past all our buildings and past the farmhouse and offices, carrying the body. He didn't want me to see him because he knew it would upset me, so he tried to get from one side of the centre to the other as quickly as possible. Unfortunately, as he was halfway through his journey with a frozen dog wrapped awkwardly in his arms, he heard me walking towards him speaking on the telephone. Quick as a flash Jim jumped behind some hedges. Apparently, I stopped just out of eyesight to carry on the conversation and smoke a cigarette. Sam's body got heavier and heavier and started to slip through the blanket while Jim tried to remain still. After five minutes Jim was unable to hold it properly and lost his grip. Sam's body slid from the blanket and fell onto the ground with a thump. It landed tail first and, because it was frozen solid, the tail snapped clean off. Jim, I suspect, cursed under his breath.

Eventually, I went and Jim rewrapped Sam, taking care not to leave the tail. He finally managed to get to his car unseen and put the body in the back, and drove to the crematorium.

Jim couldn't help laughing when he explained the rest of the story.

'I got to the crematorium and put Sam on the altar there, then I placed the tail next to him,' he recounted. 'The guy in there looked at me in horror at first but could see I was flustered so he put a hand on my shoulder and told me it was okay to be sad and that Sam was in a better place. I replied, "It's fine, he's not my dog." There was a really awkward silence after that for a while as we both stood silently side by side, looking at this frozen dog with its snarl and broken-off tail.'

Jim and I became close over the years. The trips were all bonding experiences and while we had our disagreements we would never dwell on things for long. I always tried to do my best for the camera and to give Jim what he needed to make the best shows we could. The whole team were brilliant operators. Often, I would feel guilty if we had to do retakes or if I couldn't nail it.

We were filming a piece to camera on one of our trips and each time I finished what I needed to say Jim told me to do it again. He was getting increasingly agitated and I was feeling terrible, assuming I was fluffing the shot.

'Do it again, Simon,' he repeated through gritted teeth for the twentieth time.

There was a tense atmosphere on the car journey back from the location and I went straight to my hotel room that night and felt bad for everyone because I'd held things up. Several weeks later, Jim confessed that it was nothing to do with me. He'd been out with Jason the previous night and got so pissed that he couldn't operate the camera properly. The repeated takes were because he couldn't focus on the shot he needed.

There was always plenty of laughter, usually because of mishaps. On one tense rescue in the UK I was running after an injured badger across farmland and Jim was running along behind me. The badger went to ground in a thicket on the other side of a low wire fence and so I motioned Jim to stop, then went slowly into a crouch and crept up to the fence. When I was close enough to make my move I stepped over it. I didn't register that the top cable of the fence was making a buzzing noise. It was electrified and I got zapped straight between the legs.

Even Lucy got in on the action and got the opportunity to go on a foreign assignment after a member of the public brought an exhausted cuckoo to the centre. It was virtually on the point of death and it came in with a tiny radio receiver on its back, out of which poked a miniature aerial. The bird was not injured and after a few weeks' rest had recovered so we surmised that the weight of the tracker had probably worn it out. Although the equipment only weighed 5 grams, it was still a burden for a small bird. We did some research and discovered that the bird was part of a British Trust for Ornithology (BTO) study to track migrating cuckoos and discover why so many of them were dying. In the two decades before, cuckoo numbers in the UK had halved. The BTO tagged around fifty of the birds and studied their migration routes from the UK down through Europe, across the Mediterranean and then down through Africa, across the Sahara and finally to the Congo where they spent the winter before making the long journey back again to breed.

It was a really important study and by the time our cuckoo was fit enough to fly again his fellow migrants were already far ahead in their journey and resting at a location in Italy. In order to stand a chance of survival and completing the mammoth journey our bird really needed to be with the others so we rang up British Airways and asked if they would fly a cuckoo out to Italy free of charge. One of the advantages of having a television show meant that astute corporations recognized an opportunity for good public relations and to their credit the airline said yes. And they didn't even expect the cuckoo to go in the hold. It had its own seat in first class. Lucy took it in a carrier box and was then taken to a release site where the bird was reintroduced to the rest of its flock.

Hopefully, with our help the bird finished its journey and came back to the UK to breed and boost numbers. It is a difficult call when science interferes with nature. Projects such as the cuckoo-tracking scheme are undoubtedly important but they take their toll on the animals involved, as in the case of our patient. I don't even like ringing birds because I have been called out to rescue swans regularly that have things stuck up the side of their rings. If things get caught and are not released they cause wounds that get infected, so generally I think we shouldn't interfere. I wonder how many other cuckoos were hampered by their tracking devices.

However, I would love to be able to track the animals we release so we could work out whether what we are doing is actually worthwhile. If every animal we released died the next day we would know there was no sense carrying on. We know that is not the case with some animals, such as the badgers we release, because people monitor and watch them. We also became involved in a hedgehog-tracking survey in Bushy Park near Hampton Court. The trackers used there were glued to the animals' spines and fell off after six months, which was better for them. The science is fascinating and I would love to get involved more but I wouldn't jeopardize an animal for the sake of it, even if the argument is that jeopardizing one saves 1,000 – that one animal matters to me. Unfortunately, most affordable tracking devices are telemetry based and not great for the animals. If they are implanted under the skin, they still need to have an external aerial, which then leaves an exit site which presents an infection risk. Hopefully one day there will be an affordable microchip that goes under the skin and can be GPS-monitored remotely by computer.

The Italian cuckoo release was a special case as, usually, we will only release an animal in a safe location near to where it was found. As I explained earlier, I am very particular about this because I believe the animal needs to go back to the habitat it knows; for example, urban animals will always go back to the towns they came from because they know where the food sources are. If you returned an urban fox to woodland, it wouldn't know how to hunt and feed itself. I have released foxes in the middle of busy towns late at night because that was where they were found. It is not our place to think we know better than the animal.

These were the messages we tried to get across in *Wildlife SOS* and, after sixteen years, thousands of rescues and numerous scrapes in foreign countries we continued to try and push home the message. We even expanded and produced another series, *The Bionic Vet*, which was broadcast on BBC2 in 2010. The series followed Noel Fitzpatrick, one of the vets who regularly donated his time to help treat some of the more complicated injuries we saw. Noel was an orthopaedic vet who used and developed revolutionary techniques to help save animals that would otherwise have been put down. Later, the idea was developed by Channel 4 and became the hit series, *The Supervet*.

Wildlife SOS was sold to other countries. We were shown on German television. We were trusted to do the right thing and, largely, Discovery left us alone. There was a constant struggle, however, to show the reality of what we did. WAF manage against the odds to return 70 per cent of the animals it treats back to the wild, which is phenomenal. But it also means that 30 per cent perish and I believed that the series needed to show that 30 per cent – that animals die when they come into contact with man. Yet it was always brushed under the carpet by executive producers who wanted fluffy sensationalism and happy endings. If you relentlessly represent a sanitized, upbeat version of the environment, no one believes things need to change. If I was allowed to show one death per series, I was doing well. The executives didn't like the covert stuff and the cruelty but to me, showing that was just as important as the positive stuff.

I argued and lost. In the end, after becoming the longest-running wildlife observation documentary on British television, there was an inevitable parting of the ways in 2013 (although we would be happy to discuss a new series). Budgets probably came into it as well, even though we managed to make the programmes with a team of just four people. We were flying off around the world on a budget of about £60,000 for an hour of television, which was not high by ITV or BBC standards, but was high for Discovery. Towards the end of our run on TV I was interviewed by one of the broadcast magazines and explained that I was fed up with the lack of integrity in television; there was no respect for animals and a preoccupation with sensationalism. In the end, I believe that the people who controlled the channel didn't give enough of a fuck, which is a real shame because animals don't have a voice of their own and they need someone to speak on their behalf.

CHAPTER NINETEEN

The Badger Whisperer

THE CAR WAS loaded up and ready to roll out of the gates. I left the centre and I checked my rear-view mirror. No one seemed to be following. It was dusk and I headed out to the secret location several miles away with four badgers in crates in the back of the car, sniffing and scuffling around excitedly.

I don't have favourites but I cannot deny that badgers have a special place in my heart. Thousands of badgers die annually. Some perish on the nation's roads, others die as a result of carelessly discarded litter, some are culled and others are brutally killed by cruel badger baiters. Many of the dead animals leave behind helpless orphaned cubs, which soon die without their parents. Each year, in orphan season, up to twenty arrived at our doors in various conditions; most are tiny and mainly they are in a bad way – sick and dying with broken limbs, wounds and infections that need treatment and surgery. It is never an easy ride with badgers and it takes a huge effort and a lot of dedication to get them fit, healthy and up to the stage where they will survive; it is a labour of love and the release itself has to be planned with military precision.

We have several purpose-built badger setts dotted around, which allow us to do 'soft releases'. The cubs stay with us for around six months until they are strong enough to survive in the wild. For the first six weeks they have to be hand-reared until they are weaned and then we break contact with them. They live in groups in the centre while they grow because they are social animals and then, when they reach the right size, they are transferred to one of our setts and reintroduced to the wild. For a while, the animals are monitored and food is left for them while they get used to their new surroundings; then their instincts kick in and they start to hunt and forage for their own food.

The setts have to be in the right location not only for security but also for practical reasons. You need the right type of soil and the right habitat. They need to be remote but somewhere safe. By law, you are not allowed to build within a certain distance of a badger sett but developers can get a licence to move a sett so we choose locations where there is very little chance of anything ever being built nearby. The setts are on private land where sympathetic individuals can monitor the badger activity without interfering. Over the years the setts we've built have gradually been extended by the residents who build their own chambers. The locations of the setts have to remain a closely guarded secret because badger baiting, which is cruel beyond belief, still takes place. Men with dogs dig badgers out and set dogs on them. Often the men will break a badger's leg or gouge an eye out because the dog wouldn't stand a chance against a healthy badger. Sometimes bets are laid on what animal will win and I've heard that bets can go up to £250,000. Sometimes it is done purely for fun, which is sick.

Badgers are docile, curious, social creatures and, after several months the groups we release will go off to find mates and start their own families so the setts can be rotated and used by newly raised orphans the following year.

Hand-rearing badgers is my pay-off. It's the one time I'm allowed to have sustained contact with a rescued animal because they need to be bottle-fed as they are so helpless when they come in and have not been weaned. I do everything in my power to make sure our orphans survive. Initially, they have to be hand-fed every two hours and it is all hands on deck for the first few weeks. As well as Stani and her badger skills, we have brilliant volunteers who will take the cubs home at night when they are very small to continue feeding. They bring them back in the day, when they are placed in incubators or enclosures with other cubs. We try to spread out the workload because you just can't do it every night; it is physical, tiring and emotionally draining.

When they are first brought in the cubs are even provided with teddy bears, which give them enrichment and comfort as they have all lost their mothers. Some of the soft toys have devices in them that mimic the sound of a heartbeat. However, once they are on solid food it is important to break contact and keep them at a distance. We do not want them to see humans as their parents. They are fed dog food and cat food but as they near release weight – around 10 to 12 kilograms – we introduce their natural diet of worms and insects. The worms are expensive and are ordered from a special worm breeder in Yorkshire. They are delivered through the post and come in plastic bags. One of the annual highlights at WAF is an event that we've christened 'wormfest', which is the first time our badger cubs are introduced to worms. We put handfuls of them in feeding trays and then watch the ensuing madness on the CCTV screens as the badgers scoff the new diet. Their table manners leave a bit to be desired and the noises they make are almost unnatural. It is great fun to witness and always heartening because, for those of us who have cared for them, it is confirmation that their instinct and hunger for a natural diet is strong and healthy.

In addition to baiters and developers, badgers are also threatened by the controversial badger cull, which is an absurd policy. The cull became policy in an effort to protect cattle against bovine tuberculosis (BTB), a disease that can be carried by wild animals. However, all the science going back many years says that killing badgers doesn't stop the spread of the disease. The former Labour government's scientific adviser, Professor John Krebs, carried out a ten-year trial which cost the taxpayer millions only to conclude in an independent report that culling badgers doesn't work. It is not rocket science: the clue is in the title – the disease is called bovine tuberculosis; it comes from cattle and that's where the issue lies. Cattle pass it to loads of other animals including mice, rats and deer. In pasture and in a farmyard what is a cow more likely to encounter: badgers or rats? All our badgers are tested for BTB before they are released and in all the years of rescuing badgers we have never had a case.

Badgers are also threatened in the wild by snares and traps, which are more common even in suburban areas than many people think. In one memorable case a few years ago I was called out by a member of the public who had an injured badger in his garden. When I arrived I couldn't believe what I was seeing. The badger had been caught in a wire snare that had tightened around its neck and slowly cut through all the flesh and muscle. It was horrendous. The only thing keeping its head on its body was its spine, windpipe and a few intact blood vessels. It was still walking around the garden and there was nothing I could do for it apart from put it out of its misery as quickly as I could.

In another incident, which we featured on *Wildlife SOS*, a badger had been caught in a snare around its chest and the trap had cut down to the breastbone. We tried to save it but the injuries were too extensive.

Some traps and snares are legal. Gamekeepers put them down to protect pheasants from predators such as foxes and birds of prey, and badgers sometimes become collateral damage. There are several types of trap. Fen traps are vicious and can take a finger off when they snap. They should be used to get rabbits in burrows but some gamekeepers set them on top of poles to catch hawks and buzzards. Gin traps are large with semi-circular jaws that spring shut. Thankfully, they are now illegal in this country but we still get some gin-trap related injuries because they can be bought online.

In 2015, depressingly, I got to witness again the damage traps can cause when we were called to an address in Guildford in Surrey. It was not a rural location. The road was a typical urban street near a school with houses close together. We were called by one of the residents who had seen a fox caught in a trap. When we arrived the full horror of the situation became apparent. The fox was caught in a gin trap, which had snapped shut on its leg causing terrible injuries. While we were there we found a dead fox, which had also been trapped in an identical device. We took the live fox back to the hospital but we were unable to save it.

A volunteer, angered by what he saw, returned to the road later in the day and quietly made some more enquiries about the origins of the traps. He asked around the area and did some detective work to discover the likely culprit. All the information pointed to one specific resident and we reported all the details to the police. We also joined forces with the League Against Cruel Sports and jointly offered a £1,000 reward for information about the crime. The suspect was arrested and admitted that he had laid the traps to catch foxes because they kept taking the shoes he left outside his back door. Most normal people would simply leave their shoes somewhere else but he thought it was a good idea to buy some traps from China instead. He was prosecuted and sentenced to 100 hours of community service.

The end of *Wildlife SOS* allowed me more freedom and the opportunity to concentrate all my energies on the charity. We embraced the internet fully and continued filming our rescues and editing the footage into short clips and features, which we broadcast on our YouTube channel. The internet gives us the advantage of being able to both show our work and deliver the conservation message to a global audience. Our largest audience is in the United States, even though *Wildlife SOS* was never shown there.

We use social media as much as we can as no charity can function effectively without it nowadays. While it is a great shop window for the work we do, it doesn't easily lend itself to fundraising. We have experts who work with us to try and monetize our social media platforms but, in truth, we struggle. One of our videos went viral and attracted over 4 million views but it didn't translate into donations. It was a video of me on a swan rescue. A cygnet was caught in a wire fence at the bottom of a riverside garden. Its father was on a wooden jetty on the other side trying to coax it out. I had to shush the adult out the way while I knelt down and untangled the baby, but as I did the cob kept coming back and attacking me, obviously concerned that I was hurting his cygnet. It was certainly funny but no less so than some of the other rescues on the channel. And that is one of the issues with YouTube: there is no rhyme or reason why things go viral. We put appeals for donations on all our material but without a secret formula and a way to turn clicks into pounds we are effectively shaking a collection tin into the vast emptiness of cyberspace. If everyone who followed me on Twitter gave a tenner it would be great, but they don't.

The internet is good for education, however, and it allows people to access information that ultimately helps animals survive in the wild. One of our most popular online services is the frequently asked questions section on our website that gives people details about what to do if they encounter wildlife that may need help. By giving the public the correct information and dispelling some myths we've been able to reduce the number of animals that get brought in needlessly. For example, it's not true that if you touch a fledgling the mother will reject it. Birds don't work by smell, they work by sight, and parents will continue to feed a bird on the ground, often for days if it is in a safe place. Mammals are different, however, and if a human touches a baby hog in the first few days of its life the mother will not recognize the scent on them and will eat them. There is a similar risk if a human touches a fawn. The mother may well not recognize the scent and reject her offspring. That is why we always recommend that if anyone does have to handle an animal they wear gloves and rub the gloves on soil or grass first.

We also give advice on feeding. I normally advise against supplementary feeding of wildlife because it deadens that animal's natural instincts to find its own food and builds an undesirable bond with humans. However, at certain times wildlife does benefit from a helping hand, mainly in times of adverse weather. Even then there are rules; bread and milk for hedgehogs is a definite no-no as they are very bad for them, especially babies. You need the right milk for the right animal; every species has its own milk profile. For hedgehogs, meat-based dog food or cat food is okay, as are meal worms if you can source them. And if you are feeding badgers, they love worms – but don't say I didn't warn you about the mess!

Manifesto

WHEN I STARTED my adventure in 1980 it was estimated that 5 million animals were killed on British roads every year. If you extrapolate that to take into account all the additional cars on the roads today it is not too inaccurate to estimate that now around 20 million animals are killed on the roads annually. Those are species extinction numbers.

Anecdotally, I only have to look at the ever-increasing numbers of patients that WAF deals with. It is a never-ending tide of animal misery made worse because this country is incredibly poor at building wildlife tunnels and bridges to help animals get around without being maimed or squashed. People may well say there are more important global issues than a few frogs being killed by pollution or the huge decline in hedgehog numbers but if you lose the bottom rungs in the food chain then you start to lose everything else above them.

Undoubtedly the most destructive force on earth is man. On my travels, whether in the wealthy south-east of the UK or the poorest outreaches of the world, the problems animals encountered were as a result of man. Different species in different countries might have been affected, but man was always the culprit.

So what is to be done? Firstly, governments, corporations, leaders and public figures need to do more. People start with the best intentions – they recycle, donate or subscribe – but usually this falls by the wayside so governments need to legislate. There have been notable successes, like the plastic-bag charge and the promotion of electric cars. There have been commendable voices too, such as Barack Obama, the Pope, Al Gore, Taylor Swift and Leonardo DiCaprio.

In 2010 I was invited to give a talk at an event hosted in the Zoological Society London's base at London Zoo. I couldn't help but see the bitter irony of talking about wildlife and the environment in a place where people paid to see animals in cages. However, the event was an opportunity to spread the message and raise awareness of WAF's work.

It took place around a month before the general election and one of the other speakers on the programme was David Cameron, the leader of the Conservative Party and soon-to-be Prime Minister. I had been following his career and had been impressed with the noises he was making about the environment. He had made a series of eye-catching policy promises and appeared to be one of those rarest of creatures: a politician who cared about the rest of the planet.

In 2006 he even famously travelled to Norway where he was photographed hugging a husky in an effort to display his green credentials.

Behind the scenes at the event I managed to collar Mr Cameron and had an interesting ten-minute chat with him about his plans and views. He was absolutely charming and reiterated one of his main manifesto pledges.

'If elected we are going to be the greenest government this country has seen,' he explained. I was hopeful. After several years of Conservative rule I am still waiting. The climate change agreement made in Paris in December 2015 was commendable but there is still far to go. Sadly, the clock is now ticking ever louder and time is running out. I hate to sound like Private Frazer from *Dad's Army* but we are all doomed if we don't do something about it. The simple fact is that there are too many of us and in the last 100 years we have taken too much and given nothing back. The planet is saying enough is enough and you can find the evidence at all levels, local as well as global.

There should be a body above politics that looks at every environmental situation and coordinates it internationally, from trophy hunting to solar power distribution. Environmental policy should underpin every piece of legislation, rather than be a sideshow. If we lose the planet we lose the very basis of our existence and nothing else will matter. There is no plan B and, indeed, no planet B.

The more I have seen over the years, the more vocal I have become and for many years I toyed with an idea that grew into a campaign that we continue to run alongside our rescue work. The campaign is called iDot – I Do One Thing. The idea is simple. If everyone does one thing regularly to help wildlife, those actions add up to something huge. The actions themselves though don't have to be huge. It can be as simple as picking up a piece of litter so an animal isn't injured by it or even just donating £1 to WAF. There are 64 million people in the UK and if everyone did one action a day, they would add up to 23,360,000,000 positive, planet-preserving actions a year. Thanks to the internet the campaign can be picked up globally and, with concerted action as part of a global movement, one person can make a huge difference.

As I've mentioned before, I never set out with a plan. Largely, I blundered through life, upsetting a few people but generally, I hope, doing something positive. Towards the end of 2015 I got the chance to leave a lasting legacy thanks largely to a bequest that was made to the charity. It came completely out of the blue and allowed WAF to embark on its most ambitious project to date.

It started with a letter from a solicitor, which informed me that the charity had been bequeathed two houses in the will of an old lady who died, leaving no family. The story that unfolded around the gift was completely random. The lady had not been involved in the charity and was not a member. She was only told about us by her accountant who happened to go to the same gym as Lou. The accountant had been on a cross-trainer next to Lou one day and they got talking. Lou explained a bit about WAF and later the guy had an appointment with his elderly client. She was arranging her will and mentioned to him that she wanted to leave her estate to an animal charity. He mentioned WAF and the rest is history.

Legacies are dying out so it was incredibly rare and fortuitous to get such a substantial gift. At a time when most charities struggle to survive day-to-day (which we still do) it allowed us the chance to explore the option of expanding to a new site. For some years I had been trying to find a plan for the future of WAF. It was not ideal having the centre and the hospital on the same site as my home. I will not be around for ever and that then calls into question what happens when I eventually toddle off. I'd built WAF around me. We were intrinsically linked but it had grown to be much more than the hobby it was when I first set it up. It had a life of its own, full-time staff and trustees, and it needed to be able to stand on its own when I was no longer around.

For a few years I'd had my eye on a piece of land nearby that would make an ideal base for a new purpose-built centre with a wetland wildlife refuge, an education centre and a new, state-of-the-art veterinary hospital in which vets could practise and also treat our patients. It would be a world first.

The legacy left by the lady allowed us to buy the land and start the process of turning the dream into reality. The scheme, which we gave the working title 12 Acres, will need a £5 million investment so there is a long way to go yet but it represents the future of WAF; the education centre will be my legacy because we have to inspire children.

The next years will be about reaching out to the wider community, to our supporters, to benefactors and to the corporate world to fundraise for this project, which is either insane or inspired. I'm not sure yet which! It will take a monumental effort and I'm hoping that the support we have been shown over the years will continue because 12 Acres is so important: it feeds into the future of the planet. We need to start protecting what we have and inspiring young people. At the new centre we will be able to educate and inform youngsters about the importance of conservation on every level. It's no good concentrating on the big 'sexy' species and ignoring all the smaller life further down the food chain. Ecosystems are holistic. They all lock together in a carefully balanced symbiotic relationship. If one part goes out of kilter, it all does.

The new centre will hopefully carry on my work and ideas long after I've stopped chasing animals around. I use every opportunity I can as a call to action to try and explain the importance of the project and to ask for donations or support in any way. I'm even hoping that people who read this book will be inspired enough to want to help and get involved, to donate and to spread the word.

And as for my future? Generally, I hate getting older and I won't be able to do what I do now forever. In the year 2000 my abiding memory was of my forty-eighth birthday and a celebration meal at a Greek restaurant. I performed a regular birthday tradition fuelled by ouzo, in which, from a seated start and in one movement, I deftly jumped from one chair to another while spinning 180 degrees in the air. I had always been able to do it. On my forty-eighth birthday, out came the chairs but I couldn't do it. With horror I realized that age was already catching up with me.

I've not got any younger. First, the strength in your arms goes, then you get slightly breathless when you chase a fox and the deer are getting harder to wrangle, too. For years, I have been looking for another rescuer who can take over from me when my body will no longer allow me to climb over fences and clamber through undergrowth; someone who can rescue animals like I can. There have been several times when a volunteer has arrived and I have thought, *He's the one, he's got what it takes*, but people have to earn a living and it's hard to devote the time the job demands. People come, they volunteer, they look good, I try to hold on to them but I can't pay enough to keep them, so the search continues.

I have a dependable team of fellow fanatics I can rely on when nature calls but often, in the dead of night when I'm traipsing through a field somewhere on the trail of an injured animal, it is just me. There are fleeting moments when I think I should give it up or slow down but I have a responsibility to the animals, to the people at the centre and to the supporters who love what we do; I can no more walk away from all the animal madness than I could walk away from my own shadow. So as long as there is wildlife in trouble I'll be there, puffing a bit more, swearing and looking to rescue another poor soul that needs a helping hand.

Author's Note

I hope you enjoyed reading this book and if it has in any way encouraged you to want to help WAF then please don't be shy in letting us know. There are plenty of opportunities for individuals, organizations and businesses to get involved in the 12 Acres project and support our vital work. Every day we try to redress some of the harm man is doing to the environment but we cannot do it without your help. Indigenous British wildlife, sadly, is low down on the list of priorities when it comes to causes but it is no less worthy. In fact, I will always argue that environmental issues are more important than any others because without the environment there is nothing.

Please feel free to write to us at: Wildlife Aid Foundation, Randalls Farmhouse, Randalls Road, Leatherhead, Surrey, KT22 0AL.

Alternatively, you can email us or donate through the website: www.wildlifeaid.org.uk. You can also subscribe to our YouTube channel to keep up to date with all our news.

Acknowledgements

Firstly, thanks to my family for your support and for putting up with my peculiar lifestyle, which cannot be easy.

Thank you to my friends for being there through thick and thin, and for always putting up with my requests for donations.

Thanks to all the staff and volunteers who, over the years, have made Wildlife Aid what it is today. Your dedication is an inspiration.

Thanks to my crew at Wild Productions who, through their professionalism and skill, helped make *Wildlife SOS* one of the best wildlife programmes on TV and also one of the most fun to produce.

Thanks to everyone at Michael O'Mara Books for giving me the opportunity to tell my story.

Finally, thanks to Nick Harding for having faith and enduring my second-hand smoke.

Index